AN INSTANT PLAYSCRIPT

# A PLACE

GW00482811

# AT THE

# TABLE

## SIMON BLOCK

London

**NICK HERN
BOOKS**

**www.nickhernbooks.co.uk**

**A Nick Hern Book**

*A Place at the Table* first published in Great Britain in 2000
as a paperback original by Nick Hern Books Limited,
14 Larden Road, London W3 7ST

*A Place at the Table* copyright © 2000 Simon Block

Simon Block has asserted his right to be identified as the author
of this work

Typeset by Country Setting, Kingsdown, Kent CT14 8ES
Printed and bound in Great Britain

ISBN 978 1 85459 488 4

A CIP catalogue record for this book is available from
the British Library

*A Place at the Table* was first performed at the Bush Theatre, London, on 11 February 2000. The cast was as follows:

| | |
|---|---|
| RACHEL | Katharine Burford |
| SAMMY | James Lance |
| ADAM | Eddie Marsan |
| SARAH | Joanne Pearce |

*Directed by* Julie-Anne Robinson
*Designed by* Bruce Macadie
*Lighting design* Aideen Malone
*Sound* Wayne Harris for Aura Sound

*None of us can help the things life has done to us. They're done before you realise it, and once they're done they make you do other things until at last everything comes between you and what you'd like to be, and you have lost your true self forever.*

Eugene O'Neill

**Characters**

*Sarah*, script editor – mid-late 30's

*Adam*, writer – late 20's

*Sammy*, runner – early 20's

*Rachel*, trainee – 19

**Setting**

*Board/conference room of a small television production company.*

**Time**

*The present day.*

## ACT ONE

### Scene One

*2.15 p.m. The present day. Conference room of a small television production company.*

*Standing at the right hand side of the room is a medium-sized table, seating up to six people, around which stand several chairs of the same sober-but expensive design. The table is covered with the litter of a lunch meeting (empty plastic sandwich boxes, plates, squashed cans, cups etc.). A multi-line telephone sits amidst the litter.*

*A television and video stand against the right hand wall.*

*A large window occupies much of the left hand wall. The view from it suggests the room is fairly high up. A small coffee table stands below the window. It is also covered with litter from the lunch meeting.*

*Shelving lines the back wall, upon which are videos, files and folders, propped up and weighted down by a couple of what appear to be rather obscure industry awards – nothing very recognisable. Also against the back wall stands a small tea-crate with soft packing material spilling over the top.*

*In essence the image the room projects is of a company that takes itself seriously, but isn't flashy or overflowing with money.*

*Upstage right is an opaque glass door, closed. At lights up voices are heard approaching the door. The door is almost immediately opened by RACHEL, talking, and holding the door open for ADAM, who enters in a wheelchair.*

*RACHEL:* You must say if I've offended you.
*ADAM:* You haven't.
*RACHEL:* If I did, you must.
*ADAM:* But you didn't.

*RACHEL starts tidying the debris from the lunch meeting.*

*RACHEL:* You're being nice. I can tell when someone's being nice.

*ADAM:* I'm not being nice. I'm not a *being nice* person.

*RACHEL:* I thought you had a certain look when I opened the door.

*ADAM:* No.

*RACHEL:* I thought perhaps you had a . . . a *look*.

*ADAM:* I don't find them particularly productive.

*RACHEL:* Maybe you're not aware of having it.

*ADAM:* I am. And I didn't.

*RACHEL:* I'm not meaning to offend you.

*ADAM:* I'm not offended.

*RACHEL:* I don't set out to cause offence.

*ADAM:* I've not taken any.

*RACHEL:* I mean . . . I know the words, of course.

*ADAM:* The words? I'm sorry?

*RACHEL:* The bad words.

*ADAM:* The "bad" words.

*RACHEL:* Spas, yid, nigger, paki, poof, dyke, flid, chink, mick, div, whore, cunt. I mean . . . even my grandmother –

*ADAM:* Your grandmother?

*RACHEL:* Even she knows to keep her mouth closed on certain, uh, *terminology*. But someone like me opening the door for someone like you. How would I know if that's caused offence? I see a closed door I'll open it. But that's me all over.

*ADAM:* Look, Rebecca –

*RACHEL:* Rachel.

*ADAM:* Sorry, Rachel. Look –

*RACHEL:* *Rach'* to my friends . . . and people I haven't offended.

*ADAM:* [*Beat*] Look, Rachel –

*RACHEL:* (I knew I'd offended you . . . )

*ADAM:* You simply opened a door for me.

*RACHEL:* Yes, but did I ask if you wanted it opened?

*ADAM:* How else could I've passed through it?

*RACHEL:* [*Beat*] Anyway. It wasn't so much the door opening, as the handle-grabbing.

*ADAM:* The what?

*RACHEL:* I grabbed your handles. Couldn't you tell? I instinctively reached out as you went passed.

8

*ADAM:* Don't crucify yourself.

*RACHEL:* A stranger grabs your handles without thinking and steers you through a doorway without asking. At the very least I undermined your autonomy.

*ADAM:* You steered me?

*RACHEL:* You didn't feel steered?

*ADAM:* I can't say I did.

*RACHEL:* You didn't feel . . . shepherded? Guided by a hand other than your own?

*ADAM:* No.

*RACHEL:* [*Beat*] Oh.

*Pause. ADAM looks round the room in an attempt to draw this particular exchange to a close. RACHEL waits awkwardly.*

*RACHEL:* Sarah shouldn't be a minute.

*ADAM:* Does she know I'm here?

*RACHEL:* Of course.

*ADAM:* Is she generally late for this sort of thing?

*RACHEL:* I don't know. What sort of thing is it?

*ADAM:* I was told to be here at two fifteen for a meeting with Sarah Slater.

*RACHEL:* So it's a meeting with Sarah Slater sort of thing?

*ADAM:* Is she late generally?

*RACHEL:* She was on the 'phone when I popped in to announce your arrival.

*ADAM:* On the 'phone?

*RACHEL:* Everyone's always on the 'phone here.

*ADAM:* (*Looking at his watch*) It *is* five and twenty past.

*RACHEL:* I'm sure she won't be long. (*Pause*) (*Smiling engagingly*) Busy people being busy.

*The door opens and SAMMY struggles in carrying a second tea crate, also with packing straw spilling over the top.*

*SAMMY:* Don't open the door or actually *help* or anything, Rach' . . . !

*RACHEL quickly crosses to the door, but too late.*

*SAMMY:* Yeah, I'm in now . . .

*RACHEL:* Sorry.

*SAMMY crosses to the table with the crate and puts it beside the other one on the table.*

*SAMMY:* Has she offered you a beverage?
*ADAM:* Um. No. Not yet.
*SAMMY:* Only she's supposed to offer you a beverage. (*To RACHEL*) (You're supposed to offer them a beverage).
*RACHEL:* (It slipped my mind while I was apologising for manhandling his handles).
*SAMMY:* (His what?)
*RACHEL:* (*Pointing to the handles on ADAM's wheelchair*) It was a reflex action. He's being very nice about it, but –
*SAMMY:* (*Cutting in*) You must be Adam.
*ADAM:* That's right.
*SAMMY:* Sorry about Rachel. She's new. I read your play.
*ADAM:* Oh yes.
*SAMMY:* Yeah.

*Pause.*

*ADAM:* I won't ask what you thought of it.
*SAMMY:* Well, I wouldn't tell you if you're not interested in my opinion.
*ADAM:* I'm sorry – who are you, exactly?
*SAMMY:* Oh then my opinion's only worth hearing if I'm "someone"?
*ADAM:* It's just that people who like my play usually come right out and say so, unprompted. Whereas people who've hated it tend to just tell me they've seen or read it. Full stop.
*SAMMY:* Full stop?
*ADAM:* It's like their refusal to elaborate's an invitation for me to press them further. Like I should be eager to hear their damning critique. Which – frankly – I'm not.
*SAMMY:* Nobody likes being told they're not quite as mustard as they like to think.
*ADAM:* Oh I don't mind being told my play's shit. I'm just fucked if I'm going to give some arse the *pleasure* of telling me.
*SAMMY:* [*Beat*] Um . . . for what it's worth . . . I enjoyed it.
*ADAM:* You don't have to say that.
*SAMMY:* I know. But I did. Very much.
*ADAM:* Well. That's very kind of you to say so.

*SAMMY:* You must be here to see Sarah.

*ADAM:* Why must I?

*SAMMY:* Sarah does all the playwrights.

*ADAM:* When you say "does" . . . ?

*SAMMY:* [*Beat*] (*To RACHEL*) Offer Adam a beverage, while I bring up the last box.

*SAMMY exits.*

*RACHEL:* Can I offer you something to drink? Obviously we have tea and coffee.

*ADAM:* Who was that?

*RACHEL:* That was Sammy. He's the runner. I'm kind of his trainee. Well, not kind of. I'm his trainee. He runs, I jog lightly behind, paying rapt attention as he fetches and carries. So what would you like?

*ADAM:* Actually I need the toilet.

*RACHEL:* The toilet?

*ADAM:* I expect I'm more nervous than I usually am in this type of situation 'cause I've never actually been in this type of situation before.

*RACHEL:* I'm sure there's no need to be nervous. After all . . . they called you.

*ADAM:* Even so . . . theatre's one thing, while television – whichever way you look at it – is something else entirely.

*RACHEL:* I usually look at it from the front.

*ADAM:* Not that it's television *per se*. More the act of being approached by people like Sarah Slater – whoever Sarah Slater happens to be.

*RACHEL:* Sarah's a script editor.

*ADAM:* So to be called into places like this, by people like Sarah – or indeed – by Sarah *herself*. To discuss – or simply *to talk over* – or even *around* – something that may – or *may not* – go on here. I'm only saying for me it's not a small thing. I'd even go further and say it's actually a pretty big thing.

*RACHEL:* I can see you're pretty pumped up.

*ADAM:* If you pushed me I might even say it's more or less *everything*.

*RACHEL:* Everything? Really?

*ADAM:* When my agent called about today – because I just wrote the play and submitted it to the theatre's *Marginal Voices* season, and that was just more or less that. Well. More or less.

*RACHEL:* I see.

*ADAM:* I more or less just did it, you see. So to not only get an agent from it, but to also be sought after by Sarah Slater. Makes me feel – in a way for the very first time – now it's actually real.

*RACHEL:* Well that's good, isn't it.

*ADAM:* It's one thing to promote yourself as this or that. But I've always believed until others approach us in this or that capacity it's largely irrelevant how we regard ourselves. If not irrelevant, then certainly academic.

*RACHEL:* Aren't you being a little hard on yourself?

*ADAM:* *[Beat]* No. But here I am. Sarah Slater approached me, so now I can hold up my hands and call myself a writer *to my face.*

*RACHEL:* I'm sure you could before.

*ADAM:* No. This is the point. The point is . . . I *couldn't.* So look. I'll have a quick whiz and calm down, while Sarah finishes on the 'phone. I'm assuming there is a lavatory here?

*RACHEL:* Don't be ridiculous, of course – oh . . . I see. No, no there is . . . *only* . . .

*ADAM:* Only . . . ?

*RACHEL:* Only it's a little out of the way.

*ADAM:* All you have to do is point me in the right direction.

*RACHEL:* It's probably easier if I took you.

*ADAM:* I'm sure I can find it.

*RACHEL:* I'm sure you could. It's just you'd find it quicker if I show you where it is.

*ADAM:* All I need is to be told. *[Beat]* Rachel.

*Pause.*

*RACHEL:* Okay. Back to reception. Take a left. End of that corridor take a right. End of that corridor right again. All the way to the end, take a left. First on the right. Then left. Then left. Then left. First door on the right.

*ADAM:* Thank you.

*RACHEL:* Can't miss it. Unless, of course, you go wrong. Really would be so much easier if I took you.

*ADAM:* Um, who takes you to the toilet?

*RACHEL:* I just wouldn't want you getting lost.

*ADAM:* Reception, left. End corridor, right. End corridor, right. End. Left. Right. Left, left, left. 1st on right.

*RACHEL:* *[Beat]* I'll get the door.

*RACHEL crosses to the door and opens it. ADAM remains where he is and regards her.*

**RACHEL:** I did it again, didn't I?
**ADAM:** Doors always need opening, Rachel.

*ADAM crosses to the door and passes RACHEL, who keeps the door open with her foot. As the wheelchair passes she instinctively puts her hands out to take hold of the wheelchair handles.*

**ADAM:** (*Exiting*) Really rather you didn't.

*RACHEL immediately pulls her hands back. ADAM exits, and RACHEL lets the door close with a sigh of relief at having kept her faux pas to a relative minimum. After a moment her eye is taken by the tea-crates on the table. She crosses to them and gets on tiptoe to look inside. SAMMY now enters with a third tea-crate.*

**SAMMY:** Be very careful.

*He crosses to the table and puts the third box with the other two.*

**RACHEL:** (*Poking through the packing straw*) Did James win *all* of these?
**SAMMY:** About time this company was helmed by someone with more than just a talent for lunch.
**RACHEL:** (*Spotting something in the crate*) Oh . . . wow . . .

*She reaches carefully into the crate and carefully extracts a BAFTA award, holding it reverentially in her hand. They both regard it.*

**SAMMY:** Before he arrived this place was choking with dead wood. (*Apropos the BAFTA*) Put it down now.

*RACHEL carefully places the BAFTA on the table, as SAMMY moves each crate against the back wall.*

**SAMMY:** During his first two months James was like an axe.

The time-servers. The spent. The nostalgic, mumbling about once standing behind Dennis Potter at the BBC canteen in north Acton.

*RACHEL:* (James never says much to me. Just a brief nod when we pass in the corridor).

*SAMMY:* Didn't chop it all though.

*RACHEL:* (Says please when he asks for a coffee. And thanks when I bring him one. Which is pretty considerate considering he's won a BAFTA).

*SAMMY:* Still one or two suspiciously *inert* branches clinging to the trunk. Praying the pruning season's over.

*RACHEL:* Have you shown James your script yet?

*SAMMY:* Not yet. [*Beat*] The secret of comedy, Rachel, is what?

*The door opens and SARAH's head appears.*

*SARAH:* He hasn't gone, has he?

*RACHEL:* Only as far as the toilet.

*SARAH:* The disabled toilet?

*RACHEL:* I gave him very good directions.

*SARAH:* What about coming back?

*RACHEL:* Sorry?

*SARAH:* (*Entering*) Did you give him directions for *coming back* from the disabled toilet?

*RACHEL:* Won't he simply reverse the directions for getting there?

*SARAH:* What did he go for?

*RACHEL:* What did he go to the toilet for?

*SAMMY:* Number one or number two?

*RACHEL:* He said a "whiz". (*To SAMMY*) So whatever you people mean by that.

*SARAH:* Even accounting for a puncture he should be back by now.

*SAMMY:* (*To RACHEL*) You'd better go and find him.

*RACHEL:* He seemed very confident.

*SARAH:* Rachel, even though I've been here two years there are still areas of this building I wouldn't venture into without telling reception how long to wait before coming to find me.

*SAMMY indicates RACHEL should get going.*

**RACHEL:** He won't like me fetching him. But if you insist.
**SAMMY:** Sarah?
**SARAH:** I think I do.
**RACHEL:** (*Opening the door*) "Who fetches you from the toilet?". That's what he'll say. I've met him, you haven't. He's the sort of person who's going to feel "fetched".

*RACHEL exits. SARAH looks over at the tea crates.*

**SARAH:** So they finally arrived.
**SAMMY:** Is it true he would've gone to court to get them back?
**SARAH:** I heard they gave him twenty thousand to display exact replicas in their foyer.
**SAMMY:** Twenty thousand?
**SARAH:** You have a room lined with awards one day, next they've gone. Bound to raise eyebrows. He must be thrilled.

*They regard the BAFTA on the table in reverential silence.*

**SAMMY:** Some things speak for themselves.
**SARAH:** [*Beat*] Kate didn't think he'd get them back.
**SAMMY:** [*Beat*] Has she found another job yet?
**SARAH:** [*Beat*] I was just . . . talking . . . to her.
**SAMMY:** How is she?
**SARAH:** Difficult to tell. The signal kept breaking up. Got the impression she was on some sort of train.
**SAMMY:** S'pose she could always go back to theatre.
**SARAH:** Her six year old's due to start at *Haberdashers* next year.
**SAMMY:** Ah. [*Beat*] Better go and track down Rach' and Adam.
**SARAH:** Would you.
**SAMMY:** (*Crossing to the door*) I read his play by the way. I thought it was very good.
**SARAH:** Better on stage, of course. You can't fake the response of a live crowd.
**SAMMY:** I agree you shouldn't . . .

*SAMMY exits. Pause. SARAH rolls up the sleeve of her blouse, revealing a Nicorette patch on her upper arm. She takes another patch from her pocket, removes it from its packet, and adheres it just below the first. She takes a few slow deep breaths, as though inhaling on a much needed cigarette/nicotine hit. As she rolls*

*down her sleeve she notices her hand trembling slightly. She
buttons the sleeve and composes herself, as RACHEL and
ADAM enter, with RACHEL holding the door open for ADAM,
who enters in silence.*

*RACHEL:* I told them you'd feel "fetched".
*ADAM:* If it hadn't been for some idiot sneaking a fag I
would've been back five minutes ago.
*RACHEL:* (Mark. He's been trying to give up).
*SARAH:* I was caught on the 'phone when you got here.
*RACHEL:* (Wouldn't let me lead the way. Had to follow behind,
in silence).
*SARAH:* Can I get you anything?
*ADAM:* You could get me the wanker smoking in the disabled
toilet.
*RACHEL:* Mark ran off before Adam could finish giving him a
piece of his mind.
*ADAM:* Cunt.
*SARAH:* I was thinking more along the lines of tea or coffee?

*ADAM calms himself.*

*ADAM:* I'm sorry.
*SARAH:* It's not a problem. I mean, able-bodied smokers in
disabled toilets is – of course – a problem. Obviously. I meant
you having a problem with that isn't. [*Beat*] A problem.
*ADAM:* This isn't how I wanted this to kick off.
*SARAH:* Then why don't we pretend it yet hasn't? Why don't
we kick off anew?
*ADAM:* I'd like that.
*SARAH:* (*Offering him her hand*) Pleased to meet you, Adam.
I'm Sarah, and I adore your writing.
*ADAM:* (*Shaking her hand*) Thank you.
*SARAH:* Now can I get you something to drink? We have just
about everything. I believe we've a fridge full of diet –

*RACHEL shakes her head.*

*SARAH:* Or you might just want tea or coffee.
*ADAM:* A glass of water would be fine.

*SARAH looks at RACHEL, who nods.*

*SARAH:* Still or sparkling?
*ADAM:* Still.
*SARAH:* (*To RACHEL*) And I'll have a strong black coffee.
*ADAM:* Anything with bubbles artificially added is automatically suspect in my book.
*SARAH:* Um, well, I think you'll find sparkling's rather become the industry standard.
*ADAM:* The introduction of bubbles to previously unbubbled material is obviously a disguise.
*RACHEL:* What of?
*ADAM:* We don't know – the bubbles disguise it.
*SARAH:* [*Beat*] One glass of water.
*RACHEL:* Ice and lemon?
*ADAM:* Why?
*SARAH:* One glass of water and one strong black coffee. Did I say strong?
*RACHEL:* (*Exiting*) Twice.

*Long pause. SARAH regards ADAM keenly. ADAM regards her back.*

*SARAH:* I very much enjoyed your play, Adam.
*ADAM:* My agent said you were very complimentary. (*Reaching underneath him*) I brought a few of the reviews.
*SARAH:* Toby faxed them through.
*ADAM:* That was good of him.
*SARAH:* (*Smiling*) Not really. It's his job.

*RACHEL enters with the coffee and glass of water.*

*RACHEL:* Ignore me, I'm not here.
*SARAH:* Any sign of James? I left a message on his voicemail to stop by if he has a moment.
*RACHEL:* He's been called downstairs for an 11th hour re-casting.
*SARAH:* I thought they were cast up by end of play yesterday.
*RACHEL:* The boy they thought they had turns out can't film on the Sabbath.
*SARAH:* (*To ADAM*) James is casting his first pilot since taking over. He needs a young boy who can eat a lot of cheese in under a minute.

17

*RACHEL:* It's a hilarious cheese routine.
*SARAH:* With the hilarity in the actual consumption.
*RACHEL:* Is there anything else I can get you?
*SARAH:* Adam?
*ADAM:* I'm fine, thanks.
*RACHEL:* Sarah?
*SARAH:* Could I have a biscuit with my coffee.
*RACHEL:* Digestive, shortbread, Garibaldi or Bourbon?
*SARAH:* Digestive.
*RACHEL:* Oatmeal or Rich Tea?
*SARAH:* Oatmeal.
*RACHEL:* With chocolate or without?
*SARAH:* Um . . . with.
*RACHEL:* Would that be milk chocolate or plain?
*SARAH:* Plain.
*RACHEL:* Low fat or classic?
*SARAH:* Do we have to go through this every time I'm peckish?
*RACHEL:* You have a need which it's my job to meet.
*SARAH:* I just want *a biscuit*, Rachel.
*RACHEL:* But would that be a *low fat* biscuit, or a *classic* biscuit?
*SARAH:* [*Beat*] That would be a *classic* biscuit.
*RACHEL:* A classic digestive oatmeal plain chocolate biscuit.
Now. How many?
*SARAH:* One. No. Go mad. Two.

*RACHEL exits.*

*ADAM:* She's very serious about elevenses.
*SARAH:* If you had four A-levels and a deferred scholarship to
Oxford wouldn't you find some way to jazz up waiting table?
*ADAM:* Oxford?
*SARAH:* One of our line producers met her diving in Belize
during her gap year. They got talking over a flipper and he
invited her to knock round here for a month or two.
*ADAM:* What's she going on to study?
*SARAH:* I believe it's Art History.
*ADAM:* Must be good fun, working here for a spell.
*SARAH:* Less than you'd think.
*ADAM:* I meant mixing with stars sort of thing.
*SARAH:* Mixing with stars sort of thing probably accounts for
1% of our working life.
*ADAM:* That little?

*SARAH:* And you'd be amazed how quickly the "mixing with stars sort of thing" pales besides the "being able to afford your first home sort of thing".

*ADAM:* Sure.

*SARAH:* So. Toby told you to come and see us.

*ADAM:* Us?

*SARAH:* By us I mean me.

*ADAM:* The way it seems to work is he tells me what to do, and I give him 10% of everything I earn to do what I'm told.

*SARAH:* Don't be taken in by his air of financial bewilderment. You don't build one of the best lists in London without knowing exactly what's what, and where, and for *how much.*

*ADAM:* He told me you'd said you hadn't seen anything quite like my play before.

*SARAH:* Not in terms of structure. Don't be offended, but *Jack's Flat* is extremely conventionally structured.

*ADAM:* It was my –

*SARAH:* (*Cutting in*) Of course. Though even for a first play it's "well made" almost in the pejorative sense. They wouldn't touch it with a barge pole on the Continent.

*ADAM:* I was going to say I wanted *Jack's Flat* to mimic –

*SARAH:* (*Cutting in*) Don't be offended, Adam.

*ADAM:* I'm not.

*SARAH:* In terms of television it couldn't be better. I'm simply saying *as a play*, from the point of view of one who spent ten years in theatre.

*ADAM:* [*Beat*] Right.

*SARAH:* What I actually told Toby was that I didn't think I've ever seen your play's *content.*

*ADAM:* The content?

*SARAH:* Though being strictly accurate I've seen work around its *theme.* I've seen so-called "disability theatre". What I've never seen before is disability tackled in such a mainstream fashion. It occurred to me while I was watching that had *Jack's Flat* not been about who it was about, well, it could've been about anyone.

*ADAM:* [*Beat*] That's the . . . that was the *entire* point.

*SARAH:* And it's precisely because I got that point that I wanted to meet you.

*ADAM:* But when you say I tackled the subject of disability in such a mainstream way, I think you're overlooking the fact that disability is my mainstream.

*SARAH:* Of course. But I meant it being a mainstream story about a marginalised character.

*ADAM:* Isn't loneliness universal? The need for companionship? The desire to share our lives?

*SARAH:* You misunderstand.

*ADAM:* It's just that it's not as simple as a swift glance across a crowded pub for some people.

*SARAH:* Because your pool is that much smaller.

*ADAM:* My what? My *pool*?

*SARAH:* The pool in which you're most likely to find a suitable other.

*ADAM: My* pool? Jack's Flat isn't about *me*, Sarah.

*SARAH:* Okay . . .

*ADAM:* Jack may be approximate to my age and situation . . .

*SARAH:* No, I see –

*ADAM:* . . . but don't make the mistake that Jack is me. *Like* me, perhaps. Similar in certain features and characteristics, *maybe.*

*SARAH:* It was a crass conclusion to conclude, for which I apologise.

*ADAM:* Besides . . . the "pool" is the same for everyone.

*SARAH:* In theory, yes of course.

*ADAM:* It's just that some of us find ourselves roped off down the shallow end.

*The telephone on the table rings.*

*SARAH:* Excuse me. (*SARAH picks up the receiver*) Yes, Colette. [*Beat*] But did you tell her I'm in a meeting? [*Beat*] She was supposed to've gone away yesterday but she was unable to make the final – [*Beat*] But you knew they took her car back last week? [*Beat*] Okay, put her through and I'll try calming her down. [*Beat*] It's not your fault, Colette. [*Beat*] (*To ADAM*) Won't be a sec'. [*Beat*] Kate, Kate . . . I'm in a – [*Beat*] At least you're not breaking up. [*Beat*] No, I meant the signal . . . [*Beat*] I know what you're going through, Kate. [*Beat*] No, you're absolutely right, I couldn't possibly know what you're going through. But things will work out. [*Beat*] They will. [*Beat*] I can say they will because I've always looked upon you as one of those people for whom the phrase "always lands on her feet" was – [*Beat*] I don't mean to be "fucking banal", Kate, it's just that I'm – [*Beat*] Of course. Of course you know I've said if there's *anything* I can do to help out. It's just that I'm in a meeting *right now* so why don't I call you back as soon as – [*Beat*] Of course I'll call you back, Kate. [*Beat*] I've got your mobile num – [*Beat*] Kate, just calm –

*The line goes dead. SARAH returns the receiver to its hook, and stands lost in thought for a moment. Pause.*

**SARAH:** Sorry . . .

*Pause.*

**ADAM:** Toby said I should come in as you had something in mind for me.

*Pause. SARAH is still working her way through the call in her head.*

**ADAM:** Sarah?
**SARAH:** Sorry . . .
**ADAM:** Toby said –
**SARAH:** (*Sitting at the table*) Toby?
**ADAM:** My agent.
**SARAH:** What about him?

*SAMMY enters with a plate of chocolate biscuits.*

**SAMMY:** *Votre biscuits.*
**SARAH:** (*Standing, distracted*) I'm sorry, Adam – won't be a moment.

*SARAH hurries out. Pause.*

**SAMMY:** Was it something I said?
**ADAM:** Not you. Someone called "Kate".
**SAMMY:** Kate?
**ADAM:** She just took a call from "Kate".

*Pause. SAMMY stands holding the plate of biscuits. He then crosses to the table, puts the plate down, and then returns to the door and makes sure it is properly closed. He then turns to ADAM.*

*SAMMY:* Could I give you a word of advice?
*ADAM:* If it's about my hair, I've tried everything.
*SAMMY:* It's not about your hair.
*ADAM:* I've cut it off, but it just grows back.
*SAMMY:* It's not your hair. [*Beat*] Leave.

*Pause.*

*ADAM:* Sorry?
*SAMMY:* Leave. Here. Now. While Sarah's out of the room.
*ADAM:* I only just got here.
*SAMMY:* Then now would be the perfect time to go. Before you get drawn in.
*ADAM:* Drawn into what?
*SAMMY:* Look . . . as one writer to another –
*ADAM:* Writer?
*SAMMY:* I know I'm *Timmy with the tea tray* to you. And I am that, it's just that's not *all* I am. I read your play, Adam.
*ADAM:* Yeah, you said.
*SAMMY:* However you regard me you have to understand I know what I'm talking about.
*ADAM:* What might that be exactly?
*SAMMY:* I'm talking about Sarah.
*ADAM:* Sarah?
*SAMMY:* Sarah's a nice person. A good person. She clears up after herself. However.
*ADAM:* However?
*SAMMY:* She's been backed into a corner by circumstance and's looking for an answer to her prayers. Hence you.
*ADAM:* Me?
*SAMMY:* I'll make this brief. Sarah will turn your – [*Beat*] The talent you have. [*Beat*] Sarah will fuck up its arse until you scream.
*ADAM:* [*Beat*] Sarah will fuck my talent up its arse?
*SAMMY:* She won't mean to but if you try this she will do *precisely* that.
*ADAM:* If I try what?
*SAMMY:* What she's called you in to discuss.
*ADAM:* But we haven't yet got round to what that actually is. I don't know what that is. Do you?
*SAMMY:* [*Beat*] I think I can guess.
*ADAM:* I'm sorry but who are you again?

*SAMMY:* I'm not going to pretend I'm your "friend".
*ADAM:* Good, because that takes a solid ten years in my book.
*SAMMY:* But as an admirer –
*ADAM:* An admirer?
*SAMMY:* Of your work. Because Kate . . . (*Sitting very close to ADAM*) [*Beat*] Okay. [*Beat*] You have to understand Kate moved into television from theatre, and brought Sarah in the same door. Kate was unable to translate her theatrical success into success as head of development here. So when James arrived he scanned the office and picked out certain people who were giving just the *appearance* of industry. Which he considered not only bad business but offensive to the medium that gave him everything he has.
*ADAM:* All I know is Sarah said she loved my writing.
*SAMMY:* I think she actually means she loves what she believes your writing might do for her.
*ADAM:* She seems very sincere.
*SAMMY:* Her sincerity is in direct proportion to the fear she might be downsized at a moment's notice.
*ADAM:* (*Moving away from SAMMY*) Look – I don't know exactly what's going on here . . .

*SAMMY gets up, hesitates, and leaves the room – returning a moment later having checked the coast is clear to continue. He hangs on the open door.*

*SAMMY:* Out there is medieval, Adam. An industry built on fiefdom. Serfs and Lords. Kate was Sarah's, so when Kate was lanced, Sarah became a serf in need of patronage. She now has to prove to James she's worth keeping, 'cause he's made his name travelling light through the business. It's partly what made him so attractive to the board. I know. I was invisibly serving coffee and Danish as they pored over his CV.
*ADAM:* You're going to have to slow down. It's only just sinking in you're not talking about my hair.
*SAMMY:* Sarah knew Kate's taste – it was essentially the same as her own. Unfortunately it earned Kate an invitation to hit the pavement by three thirty a month ago. So suddenly Sarah had better ditch all she held to be good and true and impress James before she receives an invite to the same street party. Which sounds simple enough. Until you appreciate it's nowhere near as simple as it sounds.

*ADAM:* My head is beginning to hurt.

*SAMMY crosses into the room and sits face to face to ADAM,*

*SAMMY:* Well, hold on tight. Sarah has to impress James while keeping in mind he's having to second guess the taste of the network script editors – his first point of contact with the powers that be. Men and women whose sole function is to second guess the endlessly mutating tastes of their own heads of department – whose own survival depends on servicing the focus-group predilections of the channel and network Controllers. Near-mythic entities who operate like *Armani* clad black holes, into which all projects are sucked and processed for potential production. These demi-Gods are specialists in one genre, but must now give the thumb up or down across *all.* And so it's not unfair to say that their knowledge of ours is questionable – and conclude that many of them have no greater clue what makes a decent sitcom than – say – (*picking up a chocolate biscuit*) this.
*ADAM:* Sitcom?
*SAMMY:* (*Eating the biscuit*) Sarah's locked into a chain of bet-hedging where the only person with a reasonable grasp of what they might actually want is you – and you have no say, and no power whatsoever. You've heard of Catch 22?
*ADAM:* Of course.
*SAMMY:* Double it and you begin to approach where Sarah's standing right now. Approach it, and ask yourself if you want to be a part of it.
*ADAM:* Did you say "sitcom"?
*SAMMY:* Don't make the lazy mistake that because most sitcom is unutterable cock it's either easy or straightforward. Anyone can mouth off about the theory of relativity, but let's not forget it took an Einstein to get the formula right.
*ADAM:* It's just that –
*SAMMY:* It ain't writing a play. It ain't gazing out the window for three months jotting down your "feelings" with literary merit.
*ADAM:* I wasn't suggesting –
*SAMMY:* Over a million pounds to make a single series.
*ADAM:* If you say so.
*SAMMY:* Money the writer's expected to justify in round the clock calls, and day-length meetings about a line or word. Anyone who says sitcom is laughable can impale themselves on

a sharp sense of humour because they simply don't understand the grinding mechanics involved in bringing one to fruition.

*ADAM:* Sammy . . .

*SAMMY:* Having to justify your existence every time you pick up a pencil to script editors, producers, line producers, directors, casting directors, actors.

*ADAM:* A sitcom about what?

*SAMMY:* All of the above will be on your back like knives. And if the show flops they'll cross the street to avoid you. And if by some freak of happenstance it hits? Well, then. They'll drown you in money to repeat the trick until you can repeat no other. Until you become a self-digesting shadow of what originally made you an interesting writer to have around. [*Beat*] You probably feel I'm painting a rather bleak picture.

*ADAM:* Well . . .

*SAMMY:* On the plus side there are some terrific Christmas parties.

*Pause.*

*ADAM:* You say Sarah asked me here to talk about a sitcom. But a sitcom about what?

*SAMMY:* [*Beat*] All I'm saying is do yourself a favour . . .

*ADAM:* A sitcom about *what*?

*SAMMY:* As one writer to another. Leave.

*ADAM:* Sammy?

*SAMMY:* For fuck's sake, about what the fuck do you *think*?

*Beat. SARAH enters, distracted and harassed.*

*SAMMY:* (*Standing, and immediately deferential to ADAM*) Are you're sure there's nothing you'd like?

*ADAM:* I could use another glass of water. Right now I could use something cold and clear to hold onto.

*SAMMY:* Still or sparkling?

*ADAM:* Anything with bubbles is –

*SARAH:* (*Cutting in*) Still. [*Beat*] Adam drinks *still*.

*SAMMY quietly exits. Pause.*

*SARAH:* Apologies for dashing out like that. [*Beat*] A woman lost her job here a short while ago. [*Beat*] We all thought she'd bounce straight back. But she hit the floor and appears to have stayed there.

*ADAM:* Kate?

*SARAH:* We comfort ourselves with the belief that the one thing we'll never lose is our dignity.

*ADAM:* More often stolen than lost in my experience.

*SARAH:* Difficult to imagine anything worse really.

*ADAM:* Did you manage to calm her down?

*SARAH:* The more I tried the worse she got. She no longer believes what people say to her. The line kept breaking up. She seemed to be on her way somewhere.

*ADAM:* It must be . . . difficult . . . for you.

*SARAH:* For me? I'm sorry, why must it be difficult for me?

*ADAM:* [*Beat*] Having to deal with it.

*SARAH:* It's not difficult for me. I don't understand why it must be difficult for me.

*ADAM:* Look. I think perhaps I should go. Maybe we can meet some other time.

*SARAH:* But now's the time to meet, Adam. There's no better time to meet here than right now. That's why I wanted to meet you here. Now.

*ADAM:* I'm . . .

*SARAH:* You're what?

*RACHEL enters with ADAM's glass of water.*

*RACHEL:* Ignore me, I'm not here again.

*She places the glass before ADAM and silently exits. Pause. ADAM picks up the glass and holds it.*

*SARAH:* Do you think we could possibly start afresh?

*ADAM:* I thought I already did.

*SARAH:* Now it's my turn. Only fair.

*ADAM:* [*Beat*] I didn't realise you made sitcom here, Sarah. You didn't say.

*SARAH:* I quite reasonably assumed Toby had.

*ADAM:* All he told me was to listen to your proposal with an open mind.

*SARAH:* [*Beat*] If you're insulted there's no comeback on Toby. Neat.

*ADAM:* Why would I be insulted?

26

*SARAH:* Because depending on your outlook my proposal is potentially insulting. No. Depending on your outlook my proposal is either breathtakingly offensive or stunningly audacious.
*ADAM:* Depending on *my* outlook.
*SARAH:* My outlook – I need hardly add – favours the latter. And between you, me, and that rather ludicrous little table, I'm pinning nearly everything I have on the hope that your outlook will favour the latter too.

*Pause. The stakes have suddenly become visible to ADAM for the first time.*

*ADAM:* We are still talking about "sitcom"?
*SARAH:* Not just a sitcom. The best outstrip the term and become cultural events in their own right. I'm thinking only of the *very* best. And I would like you to think only of the very best too. Because if we don't begin from a desire to produce the best work possible we have no right inflicting our lack of ambition on the viewing public. Too many do, and the schedules are packed with the drab result. Criticism for this is dismissed with the usual disclaimer that the public are simply being given what they want. As though anyone really knows what the public want. As though every creative act worth an audience doesn't derive from the selfish vision of a single individual. The point I am trying to make, Adam, is that the project I have in mind to propose to you today could stand beside the landmark programmes of the past.
*ADAM:* Wow.
*SARAH:* It might actually make history.
*ADAM:* Wow again.
*SARAH:* I'm not talking about television history, Adam. The project I have in mind has the potential to make *History* history.
*ADAM:* History history?
*SARAH:* At least a footnote.
*ADAM:* I have to say – if nothing else – I'm intrigued.
*SARAH:* Any writer worth their salt would be.
*ADAM:* So what's it about?
*SARAH:* [*Beat*] Well. What *might it be* about, Adam?
*ADAM:* I don't know.
*SARAH:* Well . . . what do you imagine my proposal might be about, Adam . . . that of all the young writers in this city . . . I should propose it to you?

*Pause.*

*SARAH:* Take your time.

*ADAM:* Toby told me you loved my writing.

*SARAH:* I've told you myself. It's true. I'm a fan.

*ADAM:* He implied you wanted to employ my skills.

*SARAH:* On a sitcom *about*?

*ADAM:* Wait . . .

*SARAH:* I'm not going anywhere.

*ADAM:* No, wait. On a project you wanted me to help out with.

*SARAH:* To *help out with*? Well. To create. To *write*. Which I suppose fits in with the broadest sense of "to help out with", yes.

*ADAM:* No – to help with – to *hire my skills* for something currently in the pipeline.

*SARAH:* Something currently in the pipeline?

*ADAM:* I'm sure he said –

*SARAH:* How can it be currently in the pipeline when this is the first time I've mentioned it to anyone? It can't be in the pipeline until I put in. And I wasn't putting it anywhere until I'd spoken to you.

*ADAM:* Toby definitely said . . . I'm sure he said the word "pipeline".

*SARAH:* Perhaps he said a word that sounds like "pipeline".

*ADAM:* I could swear he said "pipeline".

*SARAH:* Shall I tell you what we currently have in the pipeline, Adam? Two projects. One concerns a stand up comedian who's lost his sense of humour.

*ADAM:* Okay . . .

*SARAH:* Which currently takes the form of said comedian moaning humorously at his long-suffering, unamused Australian girlfriend.

*ADAM:* And the other project?

*SARAH:* The second project is a sitcom about a family business. It's at a fairly rudimentary stage.

*ADAM:* What kind of family business?

*SARAH:* The stage is so rudimentary you could tell me.

*ADAM:* Why Australian?

*SARAH:* Sorry?

*ADAM:* The comedian's girlfriend?

*SAMMY:* Because Australia's often easier to sell to than the US.

Which is important if we're looking to overseas sales. Which James says we must, now programmes should be designed to crack market the world over.

*Long pause.*

*ADAM:* You want me to write a sitcom about the disabled.
*SARAH:* Let's not be crude about this. Not "about the disabled". As in your play. Focused *around* a disabled character. Why not the character of *Jack* himself? Likeable. Witty. Mischievous.
*ADAM:* In a wheelchair.
*SARAH:* What I loved about your writing is how you drew comedy not from disability as such, but from the character's approach to life *as a consequence of* his disability.
*ADAM:* He doesn't have a problem with his disability. He has a problem with how he's perceived and treated because he's disabled.
*SARAH:* Precisely. I loved the way he flirts with the woman on the 'phone, and then asks her to his flat for supper. And all he feels he has to set up in order to present himself as able-bodied. So he can win her over by force of personality. Without giving her the willies by his paraplegia.
*ADAM:* "Giving her the willies"?
*SARAH:* I mean make her nervous. You know, the friend –
*ADAM:* The friend moving *Jack* between chairs when she's out of the room.
*SARAH:* To give Jack the illusion of mobility.
*ADAM:* No, no, no. This is important. To give him the *impression of normality.*
*SARAH:* [*Beat*] Yes. Of course. Adam, listen to me. [*Beat*] I can't begin to tell you what an enormous cultural event a mainstream sitcom around disability would be. Not merely an event. A milestone!
*ADAM:* Only your milestone will become my millstone, because –
*SARAH:* (*Cutting in*) No, listen, Adam, because I've actually given this a great deal of thought. Please. Because in the current climate there exists – more than ever – the need to highlight our common ground.
*ADAM:* What common ground?
*SARAH:* Between peoples.
*ADAM:* Which peoples?

*SARAH:* Peoples otherwise divided.

*ADAM:* By what?

*SARAH:* The actual sources of division are irrelevant because this project could serve as a metaphor against *all* division.

*ADAM:* And you think television situation comedy is the appropriate place to highlight the common ground?

*SARAH:* The perfect place, because it will slip inside where they least expect it. (*Crosses to the TV, and slaps it*) Suddenly . . . from nowhere . . . it's *on*! They can't believe what they're watching. Can't believe what they're hearing. How can they? They've neither watched nor heard anything like it before! And *then* – and then they start to laugh. Not from embarrassment. Not through politesse [*Beat*] I'm talking about the species of laughter they couldn't suppress if they wanted to. Laughter *with*, not *at*. And make no mistake, Adam. *Laughter with* has no mongoloid face. No *Thalidomide* arms, or *scoliotic* spine, or learning difficulties, or jug ears, or red hair, or coloured skin, or poor eyesight or fat legs, or thin legs, or *any* divisive features. [*Beat*] Because *laughter with* is simply the unique sound of unashamed, unshaming humanity . . . sharing its common ground.

*Pause.*

*ADAM:* Set that to music and you've got Cliff's next Christmas number one.

*SARAH:* I've actually given this a great deal of thought. If it has a pre-prepared feel to it, I apologise. But I believe in pre-preparation.

*ADAM:* You're asking me to nail myself into this chair.

*SARAH:* Some things are too important to fuck up through oversight. You should be reassured to find yourself in such diligent hands.

*ADAM:* You're not *listening* . . .

*The door opens and RACHEL's head pops round.*

*RACHEL:* Vomit!

*SARAH:* Hasn't Sammy explained the principle of knocking?

*RACHEL:* Sorry.

*RACHEL knocks on the door.*

*RACHEL:* There's been a vomiting downstairs. One of the cheese boys had a sudden reaction to a hunk of Red Leicester. The mother's hysterical and the kid looks like he's about to pass out. James told me to find someone who knows first aid. So do you?

*SARAH:* I took a course years ago, but it was mainly to cover broken bones on tour sort of thing. If he's slipped on his sick and twisted something I could probably make him comfortable. Other than that I can only suggest putting his head between his knees and encouraging him to breathe.

*RACHEL:* In and out?

*SARAH:* I suspect this is no time to flout convention, Rachel.

*RACHEL:* Right.

*RACHEL exits, closing the door behind her. Beat.*

*SARAH:* Where were we?

*The telephone on the table rings.*

*SARAH:* (*Picking up the receiver*) Now what? [*Beat*] I just spoke to her, can't you deal with it? [*Beat*] I just this minute got off the 'phone with her, Colette. Colette, you're the telephonist, so why don't you take some responsibility and *telephonate*. (*Slams the receiver down*)

*ADAM:* I hope you don't want to start again, again, again, because –

*SARAH:* (*Cutting in*) All I need, Adam, is for you to think seriously about this project.

*ADAM:* I've thought seriously about it, Sarah. And what I've thought is how seriously have *you* thought about it?

*SARAH:* Picture it. In your mind. For the first time on television ever. A genuine mainstream comedy about a genuinely disabled character by a genuinely disabled writer. Isn't it about time, Adam? Does it not set your writing juices gurgling with anticipation?

*ADAM:* It might if I understood one thing.

*SARAH:* One thing?

*ADAM:* Just the one.

*SARAH:* Of course. Anything to ease your unease.

*ADAM:* I don't mean to be crude, but I don't want to risk mis-understanding resulting from misplaced formality. So I'll be blunt.

*SARAH:* Be my guest.

*ADAM:* What the fuck do you care?

*SARAH:* [*Beat*] What the fuck do I care?

*ADAM:* What the fuck do you actually care. This I don't get.

*SARAH:* [*Beat*] Surely everyone should care, Adam.

*ADAM:* Not me. Not in your shoes.

*SARAH:* Surely everyone –

*ADAM:* (*Forcefully*) Not . . . *me*. Not me, so not everyone. The deaf, dumb and blind could rain from the sky and I would skip round them as they fell. In *your* shoes. People like me? In *your* shoes I would side-step people like me as I would piles of *litter*.

*SARAH:* [*Beat*] How can you sit there and say that?

*ADAM:* I just open my mouth and truth tumbles out.

*SARAH:* But you're talking from inside the ghetto, looking only as far as the ghetto wall. I – however – am on the outside looking in. Seeking a way to break the wall down.

*ADAM:* Very laudable.

*SARAH:* Thank you.

*ADAM:* Only why *you*?

*SARAH:* Why does it matter *why it matters*? Some things just *do*.

*ADAM:* Without a legitimate, knowable connection, any affiliation to a minority group is little more than a fashion statement.

*SARAH:* But what do you –

*ADAM:* (*Cutting in*) I refuse to be the dumb ass you're planning to ride into the Holy City.

*SARAH:* Dumb ass? Adam. What are you talking about?

*ADAM:* Oh I think you know what I'm talking about.

*SARAH:* I'm sorry, but –

*ADAM:* (*Cutting in*) What are you *after*? To take a genuine stand with the disenfranchised? Or merely impress yourself so far up your boss's arse you can watch his shit turn brown?

*SARAH:* [*Beat*] Okay. Now I would appreciate the courtesy of being told what it is you're actually talking about.

*ADAM:* Why don't you get Sammy to tell you.

*SARAH:* Sammy?

*ADAM:* Oh fuck this. Tell me your bottom line RIGHT NOW . . . or you can just call me a lift downstairs.

*SARAH:* My bottom line?

*ADAM:* Or I'm just gone.

*Pause.*

**SARAH:** [*Beat*] I had this friend . . . who fell off a rope on a climbing expedition. [*Beat*] Pulped his frontal lobes on impact eighty feet down a white cliff of Dover.
**ADAM:** [*Beat*] Go on.
**SARAH:** His personality changed overnight. He took up rugby. Broke his back in a scrum and is paralysed from the waist down.
**ADAM:** [*Beat*] You're lying.
**SARAH:** Of course I'm lying – what do you expect?!
**ADAM:** [*Beat*] Thank you for your interest. Your kind words and hospitality. (*Crossing to the door*) If you could get the door for me.
**SARAH:** How could anyone justify themselves like that? How dare you sit there issuing ultimatums.
**ADAM:** (*Waiting in front of the door*) If you could just get the door.
**SARAH:** It's ridiculously unfair!
**ADAM:** *Unfair*?! [*Beat*] You keep me *waiting*. You have me *fetched* from the toilet. You *attend* to other business mid-meeting, and invite me to be complicit in the *exploitation* of my own disability to make your name. *Unfair*? [*Beat*] Just get the fucking door.
**SARAH:** I have a question for you.
**ADAM:** (*Losing his temper*) JUST GET THE *FUCKING* DOOR!

*Pause.*

**ADAM:** (*Quiet*) "Please".

*Pause.*

**SARAH:** Who is your play for, Adam?
**ADAM:** The *door* . . .
**SARAH:** People like you?
**ADAM:** I do not *care*.
**SARAH:** Well, that's a coincidence. Because for the first half of *Jack's Flat* I also didn't care. As Jack prepared to create a "normal" facade for a woman he's only ever spoken to on the telephone, I thought maybe the entire enterprise was merely a single joke amusement.

*ADAM:* I'm deeply uninterested what you think then or now.
*SARAH:* But when the woman arrives. And you'd made her
*blind.* Well. [*Beat*] Then I thought "bugger me, this is trying to
be something *bigger*". And I started caring.
*ADAM:* You love my writing. Yes, you *said.*
*SARAH:* And when – even in the face of her sightlessness –
Jack cannot summon the courage to reveal who he *really* is, and
proceeds with the pretence. [*Beat*] I looked round the auditorium
and saw sorrow and compassion and *recognition* in the face of
the audience. [*Beat*] Christ . . . isn't it enough that we *care,*
without wasting time and energy inspecting credentials?

*ADAM remains facing the door. Pause.*

*ADAM:* Even if you are serious about your proposal . . . you
don't know what it is you're actually asking.
*SARAH:* Oh I think I do.
*ADAM:* You haven't got the notion of a clue. Disability is
slightly more than an original concept. It's flesh and blood. It's
people who could lose far more than you'll ever know if you got
this wrong.
*SARAH:* Then help me get it right.

*Pause.*

*ADAM:* I was so excited when I closed my front door this
morning . . .
*SARAH:* [*Beat*] Let me justify your excitement.
*ADAM:* I was so determined something could come of this . . .
*SARAH:* [*Beat*] Then why not let it?
*ADAM:* (*Turning to face SARAH*) Let's talk about the comedian
who's lost his sense of humour.
*SARAH:* Even as a concept it's an insult to anyone over the age
of five.
*ADAM:* The family business idea . . .
*SARAH:* As of yet there's little sign of a family and no business.
*What* family business idea?
*ADAM:* I've got a suggestion.
*SARAH:* No you haven't.
*ADAM:* There's this family.
*SARAH:* No there isn't.
*ADAM:* And they're in business.

*SARAH:* No they're not.

*ADAM:* And they sell . . .

*SARAH:* Adam . . .

*ADAM:* They sell this kind of . . . *stuff.*

*SARAH:* Imported stuff or stuff for export? Wholesale or retail? Knock-off or kosher?

*ADAM:* Fish and chips!

*SARAH:* Fish and chips . . .

*ADAM:* It's a fish and chip shop show.

*SARAH:* Only it's been done – atrociously. On radio.

*ADAM:* I don't believe you.

*SARAH:* I've heard the tapes. "Spamfritter Man". The best of Pete and Dud' get wiped, but the dire spamfritters survive to pollute the archive. This is what happens when we devolve culture to the bean-counters.

*ADAM:* Fruit and veg'!

*SARAH:* "The Grapes of Rothermere". Died painfully on the vine after six episodes.

*ADAM:* The family runs a charity shop!

*SARAH:* A charity shop?

*ADAM:* And it's a charity shop . . .

*SARAH:* Go on.

*ADAM:* And they're rivals with a more up-market charity shop on the same parade.

*SARAH:* Characters?

*ADAM:* [*Beat*] There's a gay manager!

*SARAH:* Wittily camp or mouth-round-a-cock queer?

*ADAM:* And it's called . . .

*SARAH:* "Charity begins at Homo".

*ADAM:* I'm ambivalent about titles that pun.

*SARAH:* I'm openly hostile. Listen to me, Adam. Listen to me very carefully. A significant proportion of people in this business no longer care why they're in it, just as long as they continue to be. Smart, decent individuals making stupid, vulgar programmes because somewhere along the line they lost the will to battle a bureaucracy that values numbers before words. But a play like yours. People like *you*, Adam, never let people like me forget what I *could* and *should* be doing here.

*ADAM:* *People like me?*

*SARAH:* With something to say. Because in the absence of people with something to say all we have left are yet more chefs making cheese on toast against the clock. I'd sooner gouge out

my eyes with the *Radio Times*. [*Beat*] Which is why I'm
convinced we should make this thing more accessible to *writers*
like yourself. (Within reason, of course). Because at the end of
every day what actually am I?
*ADAM:* A script editor.
*SARAH:* No.
*ADAM:* According to Rachel.
*SARAH:* [*Beat*] I'm merely a facilitator. [*Beat*] Nothing more.
Facilitating people like you.
*ADAM:* You keep saying *people like you.*
*SARAH:* Imbued with an authentic comic *vision*, and the means
to give it life. Don't look to me for authentic comic vision,
Adam. I only see the world as I need it to be. The world as it is
or *could be* exists well beyond my limited horizon. I know what
I am. Visionless, with but a single, meagre talent: to tell you
what yours is, and help bring it before *real people.*
*ADAM: Real people?*
*SARAH:* Not the neophytes who comb the fringe in search of
"The Edge". Forget "The Edge", it's a mirage. I should know.
I wasted ten years touring in a Bedford van deluding myself I
was delivering "edge" to the blunted masses. When I finally
realised the edge was merely the questionable invention of a
handful of psychologically suspect, self-referential literary
managers and artistic directors, that's when I heard the voice.
Inside my head. Asking me, very softly: "excuse me, but what
precisely is *your point?*". I can't describe the chill I experienced
when I heard myself eventually reply, softer still: "I'm no longer
sure. Help me. Please. Before I become irretrievably pointless".

*Pause.*

*ADAM:* And your *real people* are *who* exactly?
*SARAH:* People who flick on the box after a day's work and
watch what they're given because they have no idea they have a
right to expect better. Not more. Just better. Which is where you
come in.
*ADAM:* But I don't know if I want to come in. Not like this.
*SARAH:* Adam. You can bring something –
*ADAM:* Yeah, but I don't know if I want to bring it.
*SARAH:* Something to their attention they never noticed before.
You can widen their experience with your own. Why let
television be merely a compact mirror, when it could be a

magnificent, wide open *window*? In the final analysis, Adam, is it called narrow-casting? No. It's called *broad*-casting.

*Pause.*

**ADAM:** I dunno . . .
**SARAH:** [*Beat*] You don't know. I understand. And if you *did* know at this juncture I'd be alarmed by my own powers of persuasion.

*Pause.*

**ADAM:** I just wrote a little play for a small season at a tiny theatre.
**SARAH:** But maybe you didn't. Maybe you actually wrote a springboard from which to dive into something much, much bigger. After all . . . from such small acorns do much, much bigger acorns grow.
**ADAM:** [*Beat*] A disabled sitcom.
**SARAH:** Not *just* a disabled sitcom. The *very first mainstream disabled sitcom anywhere, ever!*. (*Crossing to the window*) Out here, Adam. How wonderful to see a difference we can make and then making it! How *privileged* to wrest television from the status quo and help elevate it to the position it once had ambition to achieve.
**ADAM:** I don't know . . .
**SARAH:** So you keep saying. But believe me, the timing could *not* be better. Because –

*The telephone on the table starts to ring. Without pausing SARAH picks up the receiver, hangs up, and rests the dead receiver on the table. She is in full-flow and in no mood for another distraction.*

**SARAH:** Because there's a deputy commissioning editor at – I won't mention which channel lest it unduly influence the tone and timbre of your writing. First and foremost it has to come from you. What I will say is we have it on authority he's not interested in seeing the usual faintly amusing wallpaper pumped out. I know for a fact he's looking for new comedy with both wit and passion. From a new angle. With a sense of purpose. A mandate. An agenda. If you will, a *mission*.

*ADAM:* I get the point.

*SARAH:* I sincerely hope so. Because this could be the biggest thing that happens to either of us, and it would be tragic to watch it sail past on a sea of ambiguity.

*The door opens and SAMMY enters, agitated.*

*SAMMY:* Colette's been trying to get hold of – (*seeing the receiver on the table*) – Oh.

*SARAH:* How many more interruptions do I have to endure before I can actually do some work?!

*SAMMY:* I'm sorry. There's been a..um.. "development" in the..um..Kate department.

*SARAH:* Well whatever that may be it's not *my* department, is it? It's the department of the person who answers the telephone. So tell Colette –

*SAMMY:* It's not the telephone, Sarah.

*SARAH:* [*Beat*] What do you mean it's not the telephone?

*SAMMY:* [*Beat*] Kate's here.

*Pause.*

*SARAH:* What?

*SAMMY:* I'm guessing she ran past door security. She's all over the shop. She was begging Colette to ask James to give back her old job.

*SAMMY:* What do you mean "she ran past security"? What's the point having security if they're simply going to allow people to run past them?

*SAMMY:* Rachel managed to mollify her enough to get her into your office.

*SARAH:* *Security* from the verb "to secure".

*SAMMY:* But being new she didn't realise your office used to be Kate's, which sparked a whole new outburst.

*SARAH:* Where is she now?

*SAMMY:* Locked in there with Rachel. I thought it might be a good idea for you to try and persuade her to leave before news of her arrival percolates downstairs to James.

*SARAH:* (*To ADAM as she crosses to the door*) She's been in a state of shock since she was walked out of the building four weeks ago. I don't know what I can do, but without her I wouldn't be here, so . . . Adam. Why don't you use the few

38

minutes this will take to sort out to think very hard about my proposition?
**ADAM:** I'll try.
**SARAH:** But you have to think *very hard*, Adam. Any soft thinking would be entirely counterproductive.
**SAMMY:** (*Holding open the door*) Sarah . . .
**SARAH:** (*To ADAM*) I'm really sorry – five minutes!

*SARAH hurriedly exits. SAMMY watches her leave. Beat.*

**ADAM:** She's been calling for the past hour.
**SAMMY:** She's been calling for the past two weeks. I didn't realise a person could alter so much so soon. Her highlights have all but disappeared. Must've lost a stone and a half. It's like bad luck reached inside and tore out two dimensions.
**ADAM:** It doesn't sound like she's taken to redundancy.
**SAMMY:** Like a duck to concrete, by the look of her. [*Beat*] So you didn't take my advice.
**ADAM:** I'm bearing it in mind.
**SAMMY:** Was I right?
**ADAM:** She wants to change the world.
**SAMMY:** Adam, she needs to make a big, fucking splash, and looking at you to be the brick she lobs in the pond.
**ADAM:** So . . . so . . . should I let her?
**SAMMY:** [*Beat*] I'm just the *runner.* I keep the wheels greased in one room or another, without actually *being* in any.
**ADAM:** You weren't so coy before.
**SAMMY:** I was simply pointing out the territory. Whether you choose to step into it . . . [*Beat*] I'd better see if they need a hand.

*SAMMY exits. ADAM sits in his wheelchair trying to get to grips with all he has been hearing. After a long pause RACHEL enters, a little shell-shocked.*

**RACHEL:** [*Beat*] Is there..um..anything I can get you?
**ADAM:** I'm fine.
**RACHEL:** Okay.
**ADAM:** Thanks.
**RACHEL:** Okay.
**ADAM:** [*Beat*] How's it going?
**RACHEL:** I tried giving her a hug.

*ADAM:* And?
*RACHEL:* Not good.

*Pause.*

*ADAM:* Rachel. When you met me at the lift . . .
*RACHEL:* What?
*ADAM:* When I arrived and you met me at the lift on this
floor . . .
*RACHEL:* What about it?
*ADAM:* What was your first impression?
*RACHEL:* I don't understand . . .
*ADAM:* Everyone makes a first impression.
*RACHEL:* So?
*ADAM:* Mine of you was *clever girl in a stupid job.* So what
was yours of me?
*RACHEL:* [*Beat*] In all honesty?
*ADAM:* In utter and complete honesty.
*RACHEL:* [*Beat*] Well . . .
*ADAM:* In absolute and total honesty.
*RACHEL:* [*Pause*] The wheelchair.
*ADAM:* [*Beat*] Thank you.
*RACHEL:* But that doesn't mean –
*ADAM:* No, I *know.* And it's fine. It's fine. With everyone there
has to be something.
*RACHEL:* I'm sorry to be so . . . *obvious.*
*ADAM:* What could be more obvious than a chair and four
wheels?
*RACHEL:* Well, I suppose a chair and four Catherine wheels.

*ADAM smiles. Beat.*

*ADAM:* (*Applies the brake to the wheelchair*) When I was
seventeen . . . (*plants his hands firmly on the armrests of the
chair*) . . . I had to go to hospital for a couple of weeks. (*He
starts to very slowly push himself up off the chair*) They wanted
to try a new course of physio. (*Standing out of the chair, with
one hand gently resting on it for balance more than support*)
And my sister gave me a . . . diary.
*RACHEL:* A diary?
*ADAM:* An empty diary. To write in. For company.

*He starts to walk very slowly and deliberately toward his glass of water on the table.*

**ADAM:** I started by writing down what I had for breakfast, lunch, supper – glorified lists really. Boy's stuff.
**RACHEL:** (*Moving a single step towards him*) Can I . . . get you anything?
**ADAM:** Nothing I can't get myself. So over the first week the stuff I wrote began to get a little bit more interesting. What I thought about the nurses. My physiotherapist's hands. Other kids on the ward. I really got into it, and by the first weekend I'd made the discovery that you could not only set down a thought on paper, you could travel around inside it. Really travel. Really cover distance. I was hooked.
**RACHEL:** On writing a diary.
**ADAM:** On writing a diary. Which I continued long after the effects of the physio wore off. Through the rest of that year, in fact.

*ADAM's legs wobble a little, and RACHEL makes a movement forward as if to catch him, but he corrects his stance before she can get too close, and continues toward the table.*

**ADAM:** When I'd filled out the very last line on the very last page I turned back to the first and read the whole thing through in a single sitting.
**RACHEL:** That good?
**ADAM:** It wasn't that it was *good*. Just that something was missing.
**RACHEL:** What was it?
**ADAM:** (*Pointing back at his wheelchair*) That. In three hundred and sixty five entries there wasn't a single reference to it. And it sounds stupid when I tell this to anyone who'll listen. But it was only after reading that diary at the age of eighteen that I was conscious of recognising *myself* for the first time. Not me in the context of *it*. Just *me*.

*Arriving at the table he takes up the glass and drinks the water.*

**RACHEL:** [*Beat*] I didn't realise you could stand on your own two feet.
**ADAM:** My sister calls me a lazy cunt. (*Indicating the wheelchair*) Could you . . .

*RACHEL quickly collects the wheelchair and wheels it over to ADAM, who sits back into it with relief.*

**ADAM:** Some people fork out a fortune in gym fees to keep fit. I sip the occasional glass of water.
**RACHEL:** What was that envelope?
**ADAM:** Envelope?
**RACHEL:** You're sitting on an envelope.
**ADAM:** Oh. The reviews of my play.
**RACHEL:** Could I see?
**ADAM:** I brought them in case Sarah hadn't read them. (*Handing the envelope to RACHEL*) But my agent already faxed them.

*RACHEL takes out several newspaper clippings and begins to flick through them.*

**RACHEL:** Why have you highlighted certain parts?
**ADAM:** I was in a shit mood last week.
**RACHEL:** (*Reading clipping #1*) "*An enabling play by a disabled young writer . . .*"
**ADAM:** Why not simply "*by a young writer*"?
**RACHEL:** (*Reading clipping #2*) "*Jack's Flat by the wheelchair bound playwright –* "
**ADAM:** (*Interrupting*) Not, simply "*by the playwright*".
**RACHEL:** (*Reading clipping #3*) "*This effective, affecting play about living with disability is all the more poignant for the fact that its author is himself disabled*".
**ADAM:** See – why should it be all the more poignant for the fact I'm disabled?
**RACHEL:** Well . . .
**ADAM:** Was *The Caretaker* less poignant 'cause Pinter never was one? Would *The Birthday Party* be less forceful if he never had one? Is *don't let them tell you what to do, Stanley* only huge if Harold *had* once been told what to do?
**RACHEL:** Um . . . I'm just a trainee.
**ADAM:** It never occurred to me I'd be bottled like that.
**RACHEL:** Bottled?
**ADAM:** Like that and like this. Bottled and labelled. "Disabled writer". A specimen in a jar on the shelf. I just wanted to be *a writer*. That's all I want. Shit . . . where am I supposed to go from here?

*SAMMY enters the room.*

**SAMMY:** She's gone.
**RACHEL:** How was she when she left?
**SAMMY:** "When she left" implies she went of her own accord. Security tracked her down and removed her by force.
**RACHEL:** By force?
**SAMMY:** Blue sky was clearly visible between the soles of her shoes and the marble floor tiles.
**RACHEL:** Didn't Sarah stop them?
**SAMMY:** [*Beat*] Sarah watched them take Kate down. Affiliate with the dead you become the dead. She was visibly shaken. But what could she do?
**RACHEL:** I can't believe she did *nothing*.
**ADAM:** Fuckit. I'm gonna leave before Sarah comes back.
**RACHEL:** Perhaps you should wait.
**ADAM:** Tell her . . . just tell her thank but no thanks.
**SAMMY:** Thanks but no thanks.
**ADAM:** Thanks but no thanks.
**SAMMY:** I'll tell her that.
**ADAM:** Thanks.
**SAMMY:** But no thanks.
**ADAM:** Thank you.
**SAMMY:** At the end of your play. [*Beat*] After Jack's sham. When the blind girl finally asks if she can run her fingers over his features to get a sense of who he is. And her hands pass over his face, down his chest and torso, onto his legs, and eventually discover the wheelchair he's now sitting in. A.k.a. the matchgirl in *City Lights* . . .
**ADAM:** [*Beat*] So?
**SAMMY:** The moment between them when there's nothing left to pretend. One human being to another.
**ADAM:** Yeah . . .
**SAMMY:** One writer to another. What happens after the end?
**ADAM:** One writer to another?
**SAMMY:** One writer to another.
**ADAM:** I like to think they go at it like rabbits and live happily ever after.
**SAMMY:** But he's paralysed from the waist down.
**ADAM:** I'll send you some literature. I'll find my own way out.
**RACHEL:** I wouldn't show you to the lift if you paid me.

*RACHEL holds the door open. ADAM exits. RACHEL lets the door swing closed. Pause.*

**RACHEL:** Sarah won't be happy.
**ADAM:** No-one who does what she does deserves to be.
**RACHEL:** She was only doing her job.
**ADAM:** Sarah's job boils down to doing whatever it takes to keep Sarah's job. Since when was that a good enough reason to be here?

*The door suddenly opens and SARAH angrily enters.*

**SARAH:** What did you say to him?! He said you'd said something earlier and now he's gone and I want to know *exactly* what that was.
**SAMMY:** Whatever I may or may not've said. Whenever I may or may not've said it. I got the very clear impression you'd already said more than enough.
**SARAH:** [*Beat*] What?
**SAMMY:** I said –
**SARAH:** Who the *fuck* do you think you are?
**SAMMY:** (*To RACHEL apropos the crates on the floor*) You can start unpacking them now. But be extremely careful. (*Crossing to the door*) I'll be downstairs with James.
**SARAH:** I just asked who the fuck you think you are?!
**SAMMY:** (*Stops*) [*Beat*] I'm a no-one hopefully on his way to being a someone. [*Beat*] What. About. *You*? (*To RACHEL, on his way out*) (Secret of comedy, Rach'?)
**RACHEL:** (Timing.)
**SAMMY:** (*Shaking his head*) (Get your boss to read your script.)

*SAMMY exits. RACHEL self-consciously starts to unpack a box of its awards as SARAH just stands in the middle of the room staring at the door trying desperately to maintain her composure.*

**SARAH:** (*Quiet*) Come back and finish it later.
**RACHEL:** But Sammy said –
**SARAH:** (*Losing her self-control*) And I'm saying come back and finish it later!

*RACHEL stands and quietly exits. Pause. SARAH sags a little where she stands.*

*After a few moments she unbuttons the cuff of her shirtsleeve and pushes the sleeve up her arm, revealing the two Nicorette patches already in place. Her hand trembling more than before, she then takes another patch from her pocket, takes it out of its packet (which drops to the floor) and puts it on her arm below the other two. She then closes her eyes and deeply "inhales". She holds the inhale for a few moments and then quietly exhales on the word . . .*

**SARAH:** Mortgage . . . (*Inhales again, holds it, exhales*) . . . mortgage . . . (*Inhales again, holds it, exhales*) . . . mortgage . . .

*She stands in a shaft of mid-afternoon sunlight with her eyes closed, quietly chanting her survival mantra, as the lights fade to black.*

**ACT TWO**

*ADAM, smartly dressed, stands in a spotlight, holding a BAFTA award. He supports himself with a stick. Beat.*

**ADAM:** It is – of course – a very great honour to be standing before you tonight. Holding – indeed cuddling – indeed, *indecently assaulting* this award for Best New Comedy series. Um . . . when we originally took *Jack In A Box* to the networks we were told by one 15 year old script editor that it would never be made. "Disabled comedy is a paradox", he said. My producer replied, "I think you mean an oxymoron". "What's an 'oxy'?" came the response. *[Beat]* When the pilot episode was eventually filmed we were informed by certain broadcasters it was unbroadcastable. We were fobbed off, put on hold, and hung up on. But we remained unapologetic, and continued to call, and eventually the network found a little spine – a few vertebrae still prepared to bear the brunt of possible failure in the pursuit of a larger success. The series was completed and finally broadcast to the nation. *[Beat]* And now I stand unsteadily before you on this – why not – on this historic occasion. Marking *History* history, not as one man cloaked in individual glory. But one of many hundreds and thousands of men, women, and children who – for as long as they can remember – have neither seen themselves reflected in the mainstream entertainments they watch, nor welcomed into the culture to which they subscribe and contribute like everyone else. So with this award I say – they say – we *all* should say – not "thank you". But about fucking time!

*ADAM stands smiling triumphantly at the audience as people do at awards ceremonies – pointing at "friends" in the crowd, and waving back at the euphoric reception the speech has generated.*

*The lights rise in the same conference/boardroom of Act One, as the spotlight on ADAM fades. The back wall of Act One has been turned into a wall solely for the tasteful display of JAMES' awards, now on glass shelves, picked out beautifully in halogen spots.*

*RACHEL entered the room about halfway through the speech and stands by the door, holding a glass of still water in one hand.*

**RACHEL:** (*At the door*) Bravo.

*ADAM jumps a little in surprise, almost dropping the BAFTA.*

**RACHEL:** (*Entering the room proper*) Or do I mean "hear, hear"? I never know with speeches – which is why I usually just bang a piece of cutlery on the table like a chimp at a tea party. Either way, well done.
**ADAM:** I hadn't finished. I didn't thank everyone.
**RACHEL:** Thank them in private. No-one likes a windbag. 'Specially one rubbing their nose in it.
**ADAM:** Was I rubbing their nose?
**RACHEL:** Let's just say . . . you seemed to be *enjoying yourself.*
**ADAM:** You think I shouldn't?
**RACHEL:** I think you probably should, but without appearing that you actually are. Earnest is good. Just enough to accept *this* award, without appearing to care for them in general.
**ADAM:** I'll bear that in mind should the occasion arise.

*RACHEL crosses to ADAM, and swaps the glass of water for the BAFTA, which she carefully replaces on the shelf.*

**RACHEL:** Sarah shouldn't be long.
**ADAM:** 'Phone?
**RACHEL:** Out. Though her arrival is imminent.
**ADAM:** Imminent?
**RACHEL:** So I've been told to tell you.
**ADAM:** (*Looks at his watch*) She did this last time I was here.
**RACHEL:** Never turning up when you're supposed to is a perk. Like cocaine – only it gets up everyone else's nose.
**ADAM:** Who does she think she is?
**RACHEL:** Sarah?
**ADAM:** I know who she is. But who does she *think* she is?
**RACHEL:** Lot of things've changed since your last visit. Lot of things and a lot of people.
**ADAM:** Didn't think you'd still be here.
**RACHEL:** I'm the Runner now.

*ADAM:* Weren't you going to university?

*RACHEL:* That's right.

*ADAM:* Art history, wasn't it?

*RACHEL:* It's just that over the last few months I've discovered I prefer moving pictures to their rather more static antecedents. Art History seems so much kind of "then". Whereas television is so much more kind of "now". Don't you think?

*ADAM:* I s'pose that's one way of looking at it.

*RACHEL:* This is what I keep telling my parents. *Now* is so much more about looking forward than back. And this is what's so brilliant about television. I mean . . . if you want to be a painter or a sculptor now you're always measured against the Caravaggios and Canovas of the past. And always found wanting. But relatively speaking no-one's made television before. You can be Caravaggio. I can be Canova. Relatively speaking we're in at the start!

*ADAM:* So I take it you don't want to be a Runner for ever?

*RACHEL:* Christ, no. I have a gameplan.

*ADAM:* A gameplan?

*RACHEL:* Strictly speaking I have a gameplan *forming*. I'm still making the mental transition from studying other peoples' creative acts to actually making my own.

*ADAM:* You're worried you might not be sufficiently qualified?

*RACHEL:* Oh no. I mean, that's the other brilliant thing about television. The main qualification for doing it is *wanting to* badly enough. Once you're in you've got to be competent at the day to day mechanics. But otherwise there's no huge pressure to show any great flair for it. Though of course I would aim to.

*ADAM:* So if you're now the Runner, Sammy's –

*RACHEL:* Just Sam now.

*ADAM:* Sam?

*RACHEL:* Or Samuel.

*ADAM:* Really.

*RACHEL:* Now he's a script associate.

*ADAM:* Sammy's a script associate?

*RACHEL:* Sam.

*ADAM:* Sorry.

*RACHEL:* Script associate and nascent writer.

*ADAM:* With which scripts does he associate exactly?

*RACHEL:* The ten or so unsolicited ones that arrive every day. He reads them and writes down what he thinks about them. A paragraph. A line. More often than not it's the same single word.

*ADAM:* "Reject".

*RACHEL:* "Shite". But should an unsolicited script contain even a sliver of promise Sam recommends it's read by James.

*ADAM:* And in the absence of promise?

*RACHEL:* They're returned with a standard letter inviting the author to send us any scripts they might write in future. With the unwritten hope they won't.

*ADAM:* But why give encouragement where none's meant?

*RACHEL:* It stops us looking like we're looking down our nose at them.

*ADAM:* But – by the sound of it – you are.

*RACHEL:* Mm. But it stops us *looking* like we are.

*Pause.*

*ADAM:* My scripts were unsolicited.

*RACHEL:* Really?

*ADAM:* Yeah.

*RACHEL:* [*Beat*] (*Professionally encouraging*) Well then that's *fantastic*. Not only fantastic, but also *exciting*.

*ADAM:* I hope so.

*RACHEL:* God yes. Samuel is *so* critical. So to not only have been *passed along*, but to have been *called in* . . . you must be *so* excited.

*ADAM:* More nervous.

*RACHEL:* Nervous . . . *of course*. But nervous *excitement*!

*ADAM:* I put a lot into them.

*RACHEL:* Naturally.

*ADAM:* A lot *invested*.

*RACHEL:* I'm sure.

*ADAM:* Both personal and professional.

*RACHEL:* But here you are!

*ADAM:* (*Allowing himself a modest smile*) I can't argue with that.

**RACHEL**: [*Beat*] Why would you want to?

*Beyond the door a ship's bell begins to toll. They listen to it for a moment. It continues until stated otherwise.*

*RACHEL:* I told you Sarah wouldn't be long.

*ADAM:* That's Sarah?

*RACHEL:* Almost certainly. With James and Sam.

*ADAM:* Did they contract Leprosy since I was here last?
*RACHEL:* No – whenever someone wins a commission or a green light for production Colette rings the bell. We all then assemble in reception to congratulate the achiever *du jour*. James introduced the idea to improve team spirit.
*ADAM:* I see.
*RACHEL:* He says the bell proclaims success for the successful, and rings last orders on those for whom success is proving *more elusive*.
*ADAM:* [*Beat*] So Sarah's won what – a commission?
*RACHEL:* The three of them were called to the network this morning, concerning a project they've been developing.
*ADAM:* A project?
*RACHEL:* Sam wrote a pilot, which Sarah knocked into shape.
*ADAM:* Sam's written a pilot?
*RACHEL:* About stand-up comedian who's lost his sense of humour. It's formula stuff, which the network finds reassuring. Plus there's a couple of half-decent parts to attract a name or two, which doesn't exactly hurt. (*Polite applause now strikes up over the ringing bell*) I'd better go through. If they're clapping they've probably arrived. James likes everyone to make a show. I'll tell Sarah you're here.
*ADAM:* [*Beat*] Thanks.

*RACHEL exits, clapping. Pause. ADAM takes a letter from his jacket, and reads in silence for a few moments.*

*ADAM:* " . . . I wonder if you could come in to talk about your project on the 15th at – ". Meaning? Rachel said – so obviously meaning . . . [*Beat*] But the stand-up . . . [*Beat*] So what? (*Scanning the letter*) Sarah's *called you in* to talk about *Jack In A Box*, so *so what?*

*The bell and applause stop ringing. Pause. ADAM folds the letter and puts it away.*

*ADAM:* Don't go looking for trouble.

*The door opens and SAMMY enters as ADAM returns the letter to his jacket. He is dressed more soberly than in Act One, and carries a half-empty bottle of Champagne.*

*SAMMY:* Well, well, well. It's true. It's you. On legs no less.
*ADAM:* A little less than legs, but significantly more than wheels. I hear you're no longer *Sammy*.
*SAMMY:* Having the moniker of someone's pet rabbit was ceasing to work in my favour. To what do we owe this pleasure?
*ADAM:* I was invited.
*SAMMY:* You were *invited*?
*ADAM:* By Sarah.
*SAMMY:* You were invited by Sarah and so you *came*.
*ADAM:* Of course.
*SAMMY:* But you *took off*, Adam. Didn't you *take off* five months ago?
*ADAM:* It was less a *taking off* than an exit stage left in high dudgeon.
*SAMMY:* Not a bad way to go.
*ADAM:* Not bad. But not clever.

*Pause. They regard one another.*

*ADAM:* I hear congratulations are in order.
*SAMMY:* (*Raising his bottle*) [*Flat, going through the motion*] What can I say . . .
*ADAM:* I didn't realise the humourless stand-up was your idea.
*SAMMY:* [*Beat*] Strictly speaking it isn't.
*ADAM:* But Rachel just told me you've written a pilot episode.
*SAMMY:* The way it works is James likes my writing, but not my ideas. His ideas – however – he loves. But a writer he is not. [*Beat*] I've landed my first series. Who am I to complain?
*ADAM:* But – one writer to another . . . how does it feel to be writing someone else's idea?
*SAMMY:* One writer to another . . . whatever gets you a place at the table.
*ADAM:* Yeah, but whose place is that? I mean, if it's someone *else's* idea.
*SAMMY:* I brought it to life.
*ADAM:* Well, you might be the *midwife*, Sammy. But he's always gonna be the father.
*SAMMY:* [*Beat*] It's Sam.
*ADAM:* What?
*SAMMY:* It's just Sam. Or Samuel.
*ADAM:* Sorry.

*SAMMY enters the room proper, staking territory. Pause.*

**SAMMY:** Unusual – I thought – to write all six episodes of a series before getting feedback on the first.
**ADAM:** I was champing at the bit.
**SAMMY:** I'm surprised your agent didn't advise you to hold your horse.
**ADAM:** I write what I want, when I want.
**SAMMY:** [*Beat*] Lucky you.
**ADAM:** You read it?
**SAMMY:** Sorry?
**ADAM:** I'd be interested in your opinion.
**SAMMY:** [*Beat*] Sarah invited you back, Adam.
**ADAM:** But you must've read it. It was unsolicited.
**SAMMY:** But you're here at *Sarah's* invitation.
**ADAM:** Why won't you tell me?
**SAMMY:** I'm not *not telling you*, Adam. It simply isn't my place to.
**ADAM:** One writer to another . . .
**SAMMY:** "One writer to another"? [*Beat*] Adam . . . past, present and future. It's every twisted fuck for himself. If you don't know that I don't think you know quite enough.

*SAMMY takes a long swig of Champagne as SARAH enters the room, carrying a pile of 6 scripts. She is significantly smarter than in Act One. More assured.*

**SARAH:** Would it be stupid to suggest you leaned a little lighter on the Champagne, Samuel?
**SAMMY:** You didn't give birth to me. You merely edit me.
**SARAH:** [*Beat*] James would like a word.
**SAMMY:** Which one?
**SARAH:** I was under the impression he wants to impart the benefit of his experience. And when someone like James wants to give someone like you the benefit of his experience, my advice is lap it up greedily. With both hands.
**SAMMY:** (*Sobering quickly*) Right. (*Crossing to the door*) You're right. I did read your series, Adam.
**ADAM:** I assumed you must have.
**SAMMY:** Very funny.
**ADAM:** Thanks.
**SAMMY:** No. Um. In the *wrong* way.

52

*SAMMY takes a swig from the bottle and exits. Beat.*

**SARAH:** Ignore him.

**ADAM:** Must feel like he's just won the F.A. cup.

**SARAH:** In truth he's only climbed into his shorts and socks, with a thousand minor disasters waiting to piss on his boots. [*Beat*] You look very well.

**ADAM:** I feel better than I have in a long time.

**SARAH:** [*Beat*] Excellent.

**ADAM:** Though how long I continue to feel like this largely – I believe – depends.

**SARAH:** On what?

**ADAM:** Well. On you.

*Pause.*

**SARAH:** I'm sorry. I'm not sure I quite understand.

**ADAM:** On your reaction to *Jack in a Box.*

**SARAH:** *My* reaction? What do you mean by that exactly?

**ADAM:** Well, after I stormed out of here five months ago I continued to storm all over for a week or so. Round Leicester Square. Into my agent's office. Down the Upminster Road.

**SARAH:** That's a big road.

**ADAM:** It was a big storm.

**SARAH:** I'm sorry. The last thing I meant was to upset you.

**ADAM:** Anyway. When I got my breath back. After I'd calmed down and towelled off. I started to actually *think.*

**SARAH:** Thinking's universally regarded as a good thing.

**ADAM:** At first I thought in general. But then I started thinking in particular. About you.

**SARAH:** About me?

**ADAM:** About asking me to write a disabled sitcom.

**SARAH:** A sitcom *around* disability.

**ADAM:** Your fervour and apparent passion.

**SARAH:** I may've been a lot of things five months ago. But I'd like to think at least one of them was –

**ADAM:** (*Cutting her off*) And I thought . . . "what if she has a point?" I didn't think you had a point at that point. But I was opening to the possibility that you might have. It took a while. And I'll be honest and admit that during that period I desperately tried to think of something to write that had no connection to any aspect of disability.

*SARAH:* Without success.

*ADAM:* It was weird. Every idea I was having had its hook in my own experience.

*SARAH:* How could they not?

*ADAM:* And after the initial frustration I began to wonder if – maybe – this wasn't a burden . . . but somehow a gift.

*SARAH:* Some writers spend a lifetime searching for –

*ADAM:* (*Cutting her off*) I'm trying to explain.

*SARAH:* [*Beat*] Sorry. Go on.

*ADAM:* You see, just before I walked out of here five months ago Sammy asked me what I thought happened between Jack and the girl immediately after the play ended. And I told him I liked to think they made love and lived happily ever after.

*SARAH:* Isn't that what everyone would like to think?

*ADAM:* Right. But after we met I realised that this makes them like any other couple in any other story.

*SARAH:* Yes but wasn't that – I mean wasn't that what lifted the play into a broader context?

*ADAM:* But they're *not* like any other couple. And this wasn't any other story. He's paraplegic. She's congenitally blind. The reality of their situation was far beyond the reach of a reassuringly happy ending. It was after accepting this that the idea for *Jack In A Box* started to formulate. An idea based in *reality* – the good . . . and the ain't so good.

*SARAH:* [*Beat*] I see.

*ADAM:* The more the idea developed the more excited I became. Like something'd lifted. Like something'd placed my fingers on a high voltage energy supply and said "get a load of that!".

*SARAH:* Hang on. So you're saying what? You're saying how long you stay out of your wheelchair depends on what? On my reaction to *Jack In A Box*? I'm sorry, Adam. I couldn't carry that responsibility.

*ADAM:* What?

*SARAH:* I couldn't possibly. No-one could.

*ADAM:* What're you talking about?

*SARAH:* You must appreciate . . . it's tantamount to emotional blackmail.

*ADAM:* I'm not on these because of *that* – don't be ridiculous. I'm like this because today is a good day, that's all. You told me I looked well and I said how long I continued to feel well depended on your response to the project I've been working on for the last five months. And it does! Wouldn't it for anyone?!

*Pause.*

**SARAH:** Oh shit. Please forgive me.

**ADAM:** You may have gone up in the world since we last met, but you haven't gone *that* fucking far up.

**SARAH:** [*Beat*] I was a little . . . confused. It's been a long day.

**ADAM:** A little more than confused if you think a few encouraging words from you can reverse fourteen years of Becker's dystrophy.

**SARAH:** I'm so sorry.

**ADAM:** For insulting me? Or making a prick of yourself?

**SARAH:** If it's any consolation I feel ever so slightly ridiculous.

*SAMMY bursts into the room, followed a few seconds later by an apologetic RACHEL.*

**SAMMY:** Guess what I just got!

**RACHEL:** I'm sorry – I tried telling him you're in a meeting –

**SAMMY:** It's only Adam. Guess what I just got from James! Presents me with a list of *five*.

**RACHEL:** Sam . . . (*Takes his arm and tries steering him towards the door*) . . . why don't you come with me . . .

**SAMMY:** (*Tearing himself free of RACHEL's grip*) I'm not talking to you. I'm talking to *them*! So why don't you fuck the fuck off!

**SARAH:** It's all right, Rachel.

**SAMMY:** See – *it's all right, Rachel.* Off you hop.

*RACHEL looks to SARAH, who nods that she is free to leave.*

**RACHEL:** (*Exiting*) I think he's been . . . (*makes a gesture of drinking*) . . .

**SAMMY:** So he presents me with a list of five, and starts crossing them off.

**SARAH:** (*To ADAM*) (Agents).

**SAMMY:** This one can't read without moving his lips. This one never reads her clients work. This one's never on the 'phone. This one's never in the country. One left.

**RACHEL:** (*At the door*) I'm sorry, Sarah.

**SARAH:** (It's all right. I'll deal with it. You go.)

*RACHEL exits.*

*SAMMY:* So James dials. Does his James thing. Bingo! Toby something-or-other.

*SARAH:* (*Picking up on the name*) Toby?

*SAMMY:* A dream of a cunt according to James. But that's what he said I need. He said "what you need in the current climate is a dream of a cunt". [*Beat*] (*Swallows*) (Shit . . . )

*SARAH:* Aren't you with Toby, Adam?

*ADAM:* [*Beat*] I was. Yeah.

*SAMMY:* (Betta sit down a sec' . . . )

*ADAM:* Until about a month ago.

*SAMMY:* (*Pulling out a chair and sitting at the table*) Think I may've possibly done too much much too young . . .

*SARAH:* So that's why *Jack In A Box* came from you direct.

*ADAM:* We had a difference of opinion.

*SAMMY:* (*Putting his head between his knees*) (Ooooh . . . )

*ADAM:* Toby refused to send you the series. He suggested I reconsider some of the writing and undertake another draft.

*SARAH:* You disagreed.

*ADAM:* What's an agent after all, but an accountant in red socks?

*SARAH:* Those particular red socks keep snug an invaluable wealth of experience.

*ADAM:* Maybe. But it's not mine. So I thought about it and came to a decision.

*SARAH:* You came to a decision.

*ADAM:* And I decided I need to be represented by someone who understands exactly where I'm coming from.

*SARAH:* But Toby's immensely respected. I mean even by people who don't respect him.

*ADAM:* He's not what I need.

*SARAH:* So who are you with?

*ADAM:* [*Beat*] I'm looking very carefully.

*SARAH:* Anyone in mind?

*ADAM:* I'm looking for someone who understands.

*SARAH:* Who understands?

*ADAM:* What it's like.

*SARAH:* What what's –

*SARAH stops mid-sentence. Pause.*

56

*SARAH:* Jesus Christ. Tell me you're not serious.

*ADAM:* After Toby refused to send you *Jack In A Box* I realised a disabled writer could only be adequately represented by someone who understood *at first hand.*

*SARAH:* Oh . . . God. You *are.* [*Beat*] Christ – I'm getting a signal that's so fucked up it can't – [*Beat*] You're seeking representation by a disabled agent.

*Pause.*

*ADAM:* On levels I wouldn't expect you to comprehend it makes perfect sense.

*SARAH regards ADAM with disbelief. Beat.*

*SAMMY:* (*His head still low*) I know I'm hearing this through a litre of Champagne . . . but please tell me our four-legged friend is taking the piss.

*ADAM:* [*Beat*] I don't take piss.

*SAMMY:* Please tell me he's got his hypothetical hands round our theoretical plonker which he is – in abstract – pulling.

*ADAM:* Are you so denatured by your dependence on James' patronage you find it impossible to believe others might have some integrity about their work?

*SAMMY raises his head. Beat.*

*SAMMY:* I just landed an *entire* series, you po-faced *ponce.*

*ADAM:* But whose series is it, *Sam.* Whose *idea*? *Yours*? Not yours.

*SAMMY:* A million pounds is about to be placed behind *my* fucking name!

*ADAM:* Your name but not your *idea.*

*SAMMY:* Fuck off.

*SARAH:* All right, stop it.

*ADAM:* Behind your name, *Samuel.*

*SAMMY:* Fuck . . . off.

*ADAM:* Behind your *hired hand.* But not really behind *you.*

*SAMMY:* (*Standing, enraged*) I've JUST been given a place at the fucking table!

*ADAM:* You have a *seat.* A seat is not a place. A seat can be added. And *taken away.*

**SAMMY:** (*Taking a step towards ADAM*) You know something. I wanna tell you something. Because I read your scripts –
**ADAM:** You said.
**SAMMY:** And you. Are. *Nowhere.*
**SARAH:** I said that's enough.
**SAMMY:** One "writer" to another: you're not even really here.
**ADAM:** [*Beat*] I don't see another writer in the room, *Sammy*. All I see is someone else's typist.

*Pause. SAMMY takes another step towards ADAM. They stand facing one another.*

**SAMMY:** If you weren't on crutches my friend . . .

*Beat. ADAM takes his hands away from his sticks, letting them fall to the floor. He then opens his arms to SAMMY, inviting whatever he thinks he can throw at him.*

**SARAH:** (*To SAMMY*) I would like you to leave now please.
**SAMMY:** (*To ADAM*) You should never have come back.
**SARAH:** Sam, I would like you to go.
**SAMMY:** [*Beat*] There's nothing for you here but misguided pity.
**SARAH:** (*Opening the door*) (*Pulling rank*) Samuel.

*Beat. SAMMY slowly walks out of the room. SARAH closes the door. Beat. ADAM sits at the table, as SARAH crosses to the telephone on the table and picks up the receiver and dials one number.*

**SARAH:** Could you have Rachel bring me in a strong black coffee. Four sugars. Adam?
**ADAM:** I'm fine.
**SARAH:** Just the coffee, Colette. And a biscuit. High fibre. Low fat. Mocha choc chip cookie with marshmallow.

*SARAH hangs up, and walks the room. She takes out a packet of cigarettes and lights one, taking a deep, needful drag.*

**ADAM:** How's your old boss?
**SARAH:** Who?
**ADAM:** Was it, Kate?

58

*SARAH:* I had a letter from her a while back.

*ADAM:* A letter.

*SARAH:* Said she was helping out at her son's nursery.

*ADAM:* Bit of a come down.

*SARAH:* No, no. Finger painting. Reading out loud. Having a whale of a time by her tone. (*Takes a drag, then exhales*) She said they have this sandpit. She said on her first day she spent all lunchtime building a sandcastle for the kids. Really ornate and pretty. She said just as she was finishing it off a little boy ran over and kicked it down. Kate said she thought she was going to burst into tears. But she said she realised it was just a sandcastle he'd kicked flat. Not her entire life.

*ADAM:* Is she trying to get back?

*SARAH:* I rather got the impression she's okay where she is for now. Plenty of sand. Plenty of ideas for castles. No-one breathing down her neck. Making sure they appeal across a broad demographic.

*ADAM:* Good for her.

*SARAH:* I wouldn't go that far. But I suppose it's better to dabble in sand than make yourself miserable in an industry you were never cut out for. Do I sound harsh?

*ADAM:* She's your friend.

*SARAH:* Friendship doesn't come into it. Remember the deputy commissioning editor actively seeking comedy with something to say?

*ADAM:* What about him?

*SARAH:* A fortnight after we met a new head of comedy was installed, installing his own people with him. The man I'd planned to approach currently time-codes cartoons for the Disney channel.

*ADAM:* So we'll take *Jack In A Box* to someone else.

*SARAH:* Someone else . . .

*ADAM:* Isn't this why you called me in? To discuss how we're going to make *Jack In A Box*? How and when?

*SARAH:* [*Beat*] If only you'd written the one episode and just sent that. A single episode would've taken a month, and we could have possibly progressed from there.

*ADAM:* I was going to write just the first and send it to you. But the end of the first became the start of the second, and the second became the third – by which time I realised I had to complete the whole story without interference.

*SARAH:* I don't interfere, Adam. I develop.

*ADAM:* It would've become an exercise in gaining your approval. *Jack* wouldn't've been *Jack.* His box wouldn't've been his box. I had to pour my lifetime into this, unhindered.

*SARAH:* I could have helped you.

*ADAM:* I didn't need help.

*SARAH:* [*Beat*] No, but I could have *stopped* you.

*ADAM:* Stopped me?

*SARAH:* I could have stopped you. And told you what I've come to appreciate since we last met. That the old certainties no longer prevail. That past tolerance of an experimental first outing is all but extinct. That they not only bury a difficult show, but have started yanking them off, mid-run. Such is the competition for audience share. And this is across the board now. Teachers, doctors, the police, banks, railways – everyone's chasing ratings now. Achievement is unambiguous in the digital age, Adam. Because a number is a fact. And a fact is – by definition – *true*.

*ADAM:* A number is merely an expression of quantity.

*SARAH:* Here, when it's big enough, it's also an expression of quality.

*ADAM:* [*Beat*] From your mouth to my ear. Even as a concept, the comic without a sense of humour was an insult to anyone over the age of five.

*SARAH:* We need no longer be good to be successful.

*ADAM:* An insult to anyone over the age of –

*SARAH:* (*Cutting him off*) Yes I heard you. And yes I said that.

*ADAM:* So how can it be worth doing now?

*SARAH:* Because someone at the network wants us to now do it. And what isn't worth doing if done well?

*ADAM:* Shit can never transcend itself. Because it's what's left after everything good's been extracted.

*SARAH:* And who decides what shit is? You?

*ADAM:* There's a common understanding.

*SARAH:* There's no such thing.

*ADAM:* There's an unspoken agreement.

*SARAH:* Says who?

*ADAM:* No-one. It's unspoken.

*SARAH:* I'm sorry, Adam. *Jack In A Box* arrived too late. Opportunity knocked, then moved on. I'm really very sorry.

*ADAM:* [*Beat*] But you invited me in to talk about it.

*SARAH:* I owed it to you in person. I owed it to your face. It was the least I could do.

*ADAM:* You set me on this path. *The least you can do* is help me walk it.

*SARAH:* Even if I wanted to –

*ADAM:* "Even"? Meaning you don't?

*SARAH:* Meaning, thinking you can change anything with a sitcom is a ridiculous, ludicrous idea I had no right asking you to embrace.

*ADAM:* What happened to "taking it inside where they least expect it"?

*SARAH:* They'll register the anomaly, and keep pressing the remote until they find that which most closely resembles what they think they want to watch.

*ADAM:* And you're now happy to supply that, are you?

*SARAH:* Entertaining the general public is a significant achievement.

*ADAM:* Surprising them would be more significant.

*SARAH:* Who are we to impose our taste?

*ADAM:* It's not imposing. It's saying here's something *else* we hope you'll enjoy.

*SARAH:* I've lived in "hope". It's no place to plant a grown up life.

*ADAM:* The essential element of even the crudest joke, Sarah, is its capacity to surprise.

*SARAH:* Nevertheless –

*ADAM:* So give them what they want and the implication is they know what they're getting before they've been given it. Where's the surprise?

*SARAH:* Adam –

*ADAM:* Where's the joke?

*SARAH:* Adam –

*ADAM:* Where's the risk – what's the *fucking point*?

*SARAH:* The fucking point is to provide twenty seven and a half minutes a week of a little welcome light relief.

*ADAM:* [*Beat*] And this is the re-formatted scope of your ambition, is it?

*SARAH:* It's like James says. The wheel doesn't need constant re-invention. It just needs to be kept turning smoothly.

*RACHEL enters with SARAH's coffee, and a biscuit on a plate.*

*RACHEL:* Sorry it took so long. Sammy's been sick. Enough va-va-voom to clear his lips, but insufficient to hurl beyond his shoes or – for that matter – the front of his suit. I sponged him down as best I could.

*SARAH:* Thank you Rachel.

*RACHEL:* [*Beat*] No problem. [*Beat*] (Sorry.)

*RACHEL exits. Beat.*

*SARAH:* Since we last met a lot of comedy water has flowed under a lot of comedy bridges, Adam.

*ADAM:* Did you invite me back to hear an apology, or a repudiation of everything you once appeared to stand for?

*SARAH:* Neither. [*Beat*] Both. Look. When Kate was walked out of this building five months ago she was begging me to help her. I wanted to say something. Call something comforting as she was escorted to the emergency stairwell. But a voice in my head said *"enough"*. *"Enough lost causes. Don't you dare move so much as a muscle"*. [*Beat*] And then I returned to this room and found you'd gone too. [*Beat*] That was more or less the final straw.

*ADAM:* Apparently more *less* than *more*.

*SARAH:* Having eluded it for so long I wanted to know what success at least *felt like* before I cleared my desk. If only someone else's. The crates of James' awards were over there. I remember unpacking them, and carefully lining them up on the carpet in a neat row. And as I moved along the row, reading the plaque on each – imagining my name in place of James' – I discovered . . . I discovered and *realised* at the same moment . . .

*ADAM:* Discovered and realised what?

*SARAH:* All the awards were for the same show. In my haste to genuflect before his prestige I had overlooked – no. I had *failed to register* the significance in the fact that he wasn't trailing a *string* of successes behind him. Only the *one*. But you land the big prize the little ones will surely follow. Topping a television festival in Germany. Winning a viewer's poll in Prague. Not a *repeated* success. Just one, and its echo.

*ADAM:* You said discovered *and* realised . . .

*SARAH:* The discovery made me realise James wasn't some media *sensation*. Merely flesh and blood running as far as his single stroke of luck would take him. So when I looked at James afresh, I understood it wasn't his success I coveted. But that *ease with himself* his success had engendered. And I understood that I needed to feel at ease with *my* self more than I needed to keep chasing the world with a match and gasoline. More than anything else, in fact.

*ADAM:* [*Beat*] I think they call that "selling out".

*SARAH:* They can call it what they like. They haven't been trying to be me for 36 years. (*Turns to the window and looks through the blind*) [*Beat*] From up here you can see half of London. Every house and flat. Every bedsit and maisonette. Every front room, lounge and kitchen. Every bedroom and study. Televisions in every one. [*Beat*] From this window you can see half the television sets in London. (*Facing ADAM*) And if just half of those are tuned into our not especially good, but not altogether awful humourless comic on a regular basis – well – my name might finally take root somewhere. [*Beat*] Is that such a terrible thing to want, Adam? To stop wandering the landscape and finally come to rest at who I might actually be?

*ADAM:* You could make *Jack In A Box* after the humourless comic.

*SARAH:* James already has my next project pipelined.

*ADAM:* After that then.

*SARAH:* After that there should be a second series of the comic.

*ADAM:* Then after that.

*SARAH:* You're talking three years from now. Probably four.

*ADAM:* I'll wait.

*SARAH:* I couldn't ask you to.

*ADAM:* But *Jack In A Box* has everything you pushed me to achieve.

*SARAH:* All I can offer you is decency without honour. (*Holding up her hands*) I'm *sorry*, Adam. Please. Can't we just leave it at that?

*Pause.*

*ADAM:* "Leave it at that"?

*SARAH:* I really think it would be best all round. We *tried*, Adam . . .

*ADAM:* You fanned the flame, and now you're scared of the roar.

*SARAH:* Roar? (*Indicating the scripts*) The writing in here rages so hard it threatens to cremate what comedy there is.

*ADAM:* *Threatens* to. Threatens to but *doesn't*.

*SARAH:* A lead character with such acute cerebral palsy he has to be strapped to his wheelchair. His speech so distorted it has to be interpreted by a care-worker?

*ADAM:* Jack is reality.

*SARAH:* It's less a sitcom than a fucking war-cry!

*ADAM:* Real writing stands up to be counted. It slaps a target on its author and illuminates their position. If I can only be accepted as a disabled writer then *fine*. I accept it. I accept the challenge. Only, on my terms. In the right hands my series would be a blast of fresh air. Fast and stinging and hilarious.

*SARAH:* Yes! [*Beat*] That's what I thought when I read it a second time.

*ADAM:* [*Beat*] What?

*SARAH:* No-one who took this job seriously would trust their initial reaction to something like this. So I read it again and then I gave it to James. I couldn't decide if it was brilliant or in the worst possible taste. Turns out it was both.

*ADAM:* James thought it was brilliant.

*SARAH:* He adored it. An incomprehensible lead. Wheelchairs a go-go. The blind. The deaf. Down's Syndrome. Autism. He was blown away by your unhinged disregard for virtually every convention of conventional sitcom.

*ADAM:* My stipulation it must be filmed not taped?

*SARAH:* Behind you one hundred percent.

*ADAM:* Well, then. That's. Isn't that fantastic? I don't understand. What's the problem?

*SARAH:* The problem?

*ADAM:* If James loves it.

*SARAH:* He thinks it's wonderful.

*ADAM:* Well then!

*SARAH:* He says as much in his notes on the back of episode 6. [*Beat*] (*Suddenly serious*) Sit down, Adam. (*Pause*) I want you to sit down. And I want you to listen very carefully to what James has to say about *Jack in a Box*.

*ADAM sits. SARAH turns to the back page of episode 6. Beat.*

*SARAH:* (*Reading*) "The dialogue is lethally good and the characters superbly realised. The satire is precisely accomplished, with the material never flinching from its spectacular assault on the cant and hypocrisy surrounding the disability debate".

*ADAM:* "Precisely accomplished".

*SARAH:* *"The writing is in turn vehement and compassionate, and the series as a whole paced to perfection. Never giving way to outright polemic or crude sentimentality".*

*ADAM:* "Vehement and compassionate".

*SARAH:* [*Beat*] *"However".*

*ADAM:* However?

*SARAH:* *"However. The subject matter is explosively sensitive. There are no lead parts an established name with half a thought for their career would touch. And reaching its natural conclusion in six episodes the project has insufficient legs".*

*ADAM:* Insufficient what?

*SARAH:* *"I cannot think of a single network – terrestrial, cable, or satellite – that would touch Jack in a Box with a barge pole. And so, consequently – with reluctance – neither can we".*

*Pause. SARAH regards ADAM.*

*ADAM:* Insufficient *legs*?

*SARAH:* Without which it can't run and run. An element of endless repeatability is integral to any successful show.

*ADAM:* They only made two series of *Fawlty Towers*.

*SARAH:* But that was *Fawlty Towers*.

*ADAM:* It wasn't *Fawlty Towers* until it became *Fawlty Towers*. Before then it was a tightly scripted farce about a psychotic, racist snob in a blazer. But someone took a gamble.

*SARAH:* Gambles are a thing of the past. Now we "risk assess".

*ADAM:* Risk assess?

*SARAH:* It's less cavalier than gambling. Less voodoo, more professional.

*Pause.*

*ADAM:* Fine. You don't want *Jack in a Box*. I'll take it somewhere else.

*SARAH:* [*Beat*] Adam. If you try peddling *Jack In A Box* you will become an industry anecdote. Receptionists won't receive you. Personal assistants won't assist you. Executives will speak of you only to relieve their stress.

*ADAM:* In your opinion. Which – as it would appear – is worth about as much as your next pay cheque.

*Pause.*

*SARAH:* I'm going to ignore that remark.

*ADAM:* Ignoring certain truths about your new self must be second nature to you now.

*SARAH:* I beg your pardon.

*ADAM:* "*Entertaining the public's a significant achievement*"? Five months back you'd've smacked yourself in the mouth for a platitude that fucking specious.

*SARAH:* I understand you might be upset, but there's no need to be unpleasant.

*ADAM:* Upset? I'm completely gutted!

*SARAH:* Adam –

*ADAM:* In your *finite* wisdom you have completely gutted me!

*SARAH:* If you'd have written just one episode –

*ADAM:* Hey – I'll write as I see fit, if it's all the same to whoever you think you are today! Five months ago you were on your hands and knees to me to come up with something extraordinary to save your desperate behind. So don't stand here trying to look insulted and tell me you don't totally deserve the onus I'm now heaping upon you. At the very beginning you came to me, remember? You . . . came . . . to . . . *me*. *Remember*?

*SARAH:* [*Beat*] How could I forget?

*ADAM:* Fucking right. So now I need to know what you're *now* going to do about this.

*SARAH:* [*Beat*] I could offer you my sincere apology.

*ADAM:* You've just dropped napalm on the last five months of my life. Your spur of the moment *sincerity* is ever so slightly *less* than what I had in mind.

*SARAH:* I think you shouldn't say any more. Because I think you're about to be very insulting, and I think I'm about to be very insulted.

*ADAM:* [*Beat*] (*Approaching SARAH and putting his face very close to hers*) (*Quiet. Deliberate. Forceful*) You brought me in here and wound me up like a toy and off I went. Here I am, back with the very goods you sent me to collect, and you look at me like I'm last year's Christmas present. If you imagine I'm about to toddle quietly out of this building like a good little *spas*, I would think – *very hard* – again.

*SARAH:* What I said then I meant then. However –

*ADAM:* However nothing. You had no right to ask me to do something when you had no idea what you were doing.

*SARAH:* I was on a steep learning curve.

*ADAM:* You wanted to use me to announce yourself. You used me. It was ab-*use.*
*SARAH:* I had an idea. It didn't work out. That's life. It's certainly television. I'm sorry, but there is really nothing else I can say!

*Pause. ADAM's tone softens.*

*ADAM:* Look. Okay, look. Listen. Give me some notes.
*SARAH:* Some what?
*ADAM:* I'll re-write the scripts.
*SARAH:* Opportunity *knocked*, Adam. There was no answer. It *moved on.*
*ADAM:* I'll make Jack more intelligible. I'll tone down his cerebral palsy. I'll even give him a love interest. Sarah, please. [*Beat*] I can't get an agent to touch me.

*Pause.*

*SARAH:* [*Beat*] What?
*ADAM:* I can't get a meeting anywhere. You've got to help me. I've written and apologised to Toby, but he doesn't reply. He won't take my calls. I think he's spread some word.
*SARAH:* The speed with which a name can be coated in ka-ka in this business is terrifying. Without an agent you have no representation in the market-place. No marketability. No future.
*ADAM:* All else aside, you called me in. I apologise for everything I just said, but that has to be worth *something.*
*SARAH:* Adam –
*ADAM:* (*Losing control*) How can you simply turn your back on this?!

*Long pause. SARAH regards ADAM.*

*SARAH:* Wait. [*Beat*] Just . . . just wait.
*ADAM:* I'm sorry . . . shit, I'm sorry . . .

*SARAH slowly crosses to the door. She turns and regards ADAM. Beat. SARAH exits. ADAM stands staring at the door. He has finally reached the bottom and is overwhelmed with emotion and fear. He starts to cry.*

*After several more moments RACHEL enters.*

*RACHEL:* I'm under instruction to –

*She stops in her tracks at the sight of ADAM. Pause. She approaches to comfort him.*

*RACHEL:* Adam. Whatever it is. Whatever Sarah. You oughtn't take it to heart. Because. Adam. Because. What I. When things. What I started to keep to the forefront when things. When a situation here gets on top of me. I remind myself. Remind yourself. Because that's what it is. All it is. It's only telly. So it doesn't actually matter. I mean, how can it? When there's so much of it?

*The door quietly opens and SAMMY enters, sobered. Sick stains his suit. Pause.*

*SAMMY:* After I took you to one side. [*Beat*] After I risked my job. [*Beat*] After I set my head on the block out of respect for you. This is how I'm repaid.
*RACHEL:* Sam.
*SAMMY:* Not you. (*To ADAM*) Tell me what you said to send Sarah into James, requesting *that*?
*RACHEL:* (*Placing a hand on SAMMY'S arm*) Samuel . . .
*SAMMY:* (*Freeing his arm. To RACHEL*) When I spew on myself, wipe it off. Otherwise, not you. So scurry back to your hutch you under-achieving, trustafarian *tourist.*
*RACHEL:* [*Beat*] Next time you laminate yourself in your half-digested lunch I will take a funnel. And a shoehorn. And stuff it back down your throat. Until you choke.
*SAMMY:* Why don't you take some of daddy's money and go buy yourself some more over-priced trainers.
*RACHEL:* (*Hurt by the reduction, but determined not to break in front of SAMMY*) [*Beat*] I'm sorry, Adam. I don't see why I have stay in this room with this. If you need me . . . I'll be in reception.
*SAMMY:* (*As RACHEL exits*) Why would anyone need *you*?

*RACHEL exits. SAMMY turns on ADAM before she has even left the room.*

*SAMMY:* The only consolation – the single factor allowing me to write someone else's idea was I would get sole credit for the series. Not quite the original calling card I had in mind for myself, but just my name at the front was the next best thing.

*ADAM:* I don't know what she's requesting.

*SAMMY:* Oh, you know what she's requesting.

*ADAM:* I don't.

*SAMMY:* I know you do.

*SARAH enters.*

*SARAH:* What did you just say to her?

*SAMMY:* I held a mirror up to her soul. It's what good writers *do.*

*SARAH:* Carry on like this and I will begin to fear for your place on the team.

*SAMMY:* Without me there wouldn't be a fucking team. I was guaranteed the *whole* series.

*SARAH:* Regard it as a donation to a worthy cause.

*SAMMY:* Donations are made by *choice.*

*SARAH:* The idea was James'. The format is James'. He who holds the format holds the keys to the castle.

*SAMMY:* We had an *understanding.*

*SARAH:* Understandings deepen as the broader picture unfolds.

*SAMMY:* I wrote the pilot that made the series possible.

*SARAH:* But James gave you the opportunity to do that. And his gratitude is genuine. But it's limited up to the point where you start behaving . . . well . . . I suspect something like this.

*SAMMY:* A promise was made.

*SARAH:* But not a contract.

*SAMMY:* My agent –

*SARAH:* Your agent took you on at the recommendation of James. They were at college together. Blood is thicker than water. Do you see how this starts to work? [*Beat*] I'm sorry, Sammy, for the facts of life being what they are. But these are the facts of life and we must live with them.

*SAMMY:* (*Scooping up ADAM's six scripts*) So because of this, I have to go from writer to *co-writer*? From writer to fucking *hack*?

*SARAH:* Sharing can be a humbling experience.

*SAMMY:* Then . . . (*hurling the scripts at SARAH*) . . . *you* share!

*Pause.*

*SARAH: (Quiet, unshakeable)* In hindsight I believe you'll appreciate that giving up an episode is not a bad thing, but a thing of good.

*SAMMY:* You fuck him over then steal from me to slip your conscience off the hook.

*SARAH:* I'm sorry you see it that way.

*SAMMY:* When I'm rich and famous I'm coming after you. Don't *ever* forget that.

*SARAH:* [*Beat*] I'll just have to make sure I'm richer. And more famous.

*SAMMY:* I'm gonna speak to people about this.

*ADAM:* You want me to write an episode –

*SARAH: (Interrupting)* We want to *commission* you to write an episode which, if successful, would be considered for the broadcast series.

*SAMMY:* (You pair of thieves.)

*SARAH:* You will then become a broadcast name. A name with which people can do business.

*SAMMY:* (You have stolen from the poor.)

*SARAH:* And you'll once more enjoy the beginnings of a career in blossom.

*SAMMY:* (Only it's *my* blossom!)

*SARAH:* In contrast to your career as it currently stands.

*SAMMY:* (In deepest shit.)

*SARAH:* Sporting a wreath.

*SAMMY: (Turning on SARAH)* What you are . . . *(Calm, deadly)* *I* love this. *I* believe in it. *I* was born to be a part of it. Most of it's shit – but so is most of everything else. But at its best I can't think of anywhere I'd rather be. But you people. Story structure manuals in one hand. Unopened *Poetics* in the other. Masking your ignorance of the art of telly with the science of "programme-making". Accessorizing your mediocrity with audience theory and "associated process" that has *everything* to do with the manufacture of "product", and *nothing* to do with the pursuit of a gut instinct.

*SARAH:* Have you finished?

*SAMMY:* [*Beat*] How quickly you've settled for what you once affected to despise. You're no better than Kate, just a more aggressive strain of the same virus. Pretend better. Smile wider, as you knife deeper.

*SARAH:* Have you finished *now*?

*SAMMY:* [*Beat*] However much money you make. However many private drinking clubs you join. You will *never* make a true place for yourself here. Because at the back of your mind will always be the knowledge that you're only here because you failed somewhere else. You make me sick.

*SARAH:* It would seem a lot of things have that effect on you. As you gain experience I've no doubt you'll learn to stomach the world better.

*SAMMY:* [*Beat*] *Fraud.* [*Beat*] Because what you are . . . is a fraud.

*SAMMY regards SARAH with intense hatred, and then quietly exits. SARAH faces the door, her back to ADAM. Long pause.*

*SARAH:* (*Quiet*) James didn't take much persuasion to agree to commission a script, Adam. [*Beat*] He thought bringing in a disabled character for an episode might be a useful injection of . . . pathos.

*ADAM:* [*Beat*] How wonderful to see a difference we could make, and then making it. How privileged.

*SARAH:* Sounds like something Kate might have said.

*ADAM:* [*Beat*] Not Kate.

*SARAH turns and faces ADAM.*

*SARAH:* We can stand and bemoan what's past. (*Crossing to the table*) Or sit down and plan the future.

*ADAM:* Sit at the table with *you*?

*SARAH:* [*Beat*] Like a lot of writers in the foothills of their career Sammy thinks in black and white, and talks in slogans. Because I wasn't born into the faith he feels I have no right to be here. Because I'm a convert. Because I'm not strictly orthodox. Because I *compromised.*

*ADAM:* Because you stitched him up.

*SARAH:* For him it's his life, for me it can only ever be my living. I already gave myself to Art, Adam. In return it gave me crippling debt and a diminished will to live. So I'm afraid I've had to swap Art for knowing where I'm going to be tomorrow. [*Beat*] The question is. [*Beat*] Where is Adam going to be tomorrow?

*ADAM:* I don't generally give tomorrow much thought.

*SARAH:* Well . . . maybe it's time you did. [*Beat*] Time to take yourself seriously, Adam. It's time to be sensible. [*Pause*] It's decision time.

*Pause.*

*ADAM:* I . . . um . . . I need a drink.
*SARAH:* A drink? Of course.
*ADAM:* A glass of water. My throat's dry.
*SARAH:* One glass of water.
*ADAM:* Please.
*SARAH:* One glass of *still* water?
*ADAM:* [*Beat*] Perhaps I should try the industry standard . . . before dismissing it out of hand. [*Beat*] What do you think?
*SARAH:* What do *I* think?
*ADAM:* What do you think?
*SARAH:* [*Beat*] What do *you* think?
*ADAM:* What do you think I should think?
*SARAH:* I can't tell you what to think.
*ADAM:* No. I . . . [*Beat*] I don't know what I think. (*He looks from the door to SARAH at the table*) I don't know.

*SARAH slowly pulls out a chair at the table for ADAM. Pause.*

*SARAH:* Still or sparkling? [*Beat*] It's your call.

*ADAM stands immobilised, facing SARAH.*

*Slow fade to black.*

END.